A Perspective on
Social Communication

A Perspective on Social Communication

Stuart J. Sigman
State University of New York at Buffalo

Lexington Books
D.C. Heath and Company/Lexington, Massachusetts/Toronto

Library of Congress Cataloging-in-Publication Data

Sigman, Stuart J.
   A perspective on social communication.

   Bibliography: p.
   1. Interpersonal relations. 2. Interpersonal communication. 3. Social interaction.
I. Title.
HM132.S535   1987   302.3′4   86-45036
ISBN 0-669-13012-5 (alk. paper)

Published simultaneously in Canada
Printed in the United States of America
Casebound International Standard Book Number: 0-669-13012-5
Library of Congress Catalog Card Number: 86-45036

The paper used in this publication meets the minimum requirements of American National Standard for Information Sciences—Permanence of Paper for Printed Library Materials, ANSI Z39.48-1984.

87 88 89 90 8 7 6 5 4 3 2 1

Dedicated to my parents,
Pauline and Harvey Sigman,
for the roads offered and taken

Contents

Figures and Tables

Figures

Tables

Preface

Social communication theory is the name of an as yet loosely coordinated body of works by certain anthropologists, linguists, psychiatrists, and sociologists who at various points in their careers have concentrated on the study of communication processes. Social communication is what Winkin (1980) introduced to European audiences as "la nouvelle communication" and what Thomas (1981) described as the "organic approach" to communication; it apparently is the result of the interactions among an "invisible college" of eminent scholars (Crane, 1972; Winkin, 1980). Ironically, social communication has not received much attention from the discipline of communication.

The current debate over qualitative versus quantitative techniques is a simplistic attempt to grapple with the "new communication" and with the few strands of social communication theory that have entered mainstream communication thought (for example, Bateson, 1972; Watzlawick, Beavin, and Jackson, 1967). For me, the important issue does not revolve around measurement and measuring instruments, but rather the very nature of the phenomena to be measured. Traditionally, the discipline of communication has taken an intending and competent being, that is, the individual communicator, as its starting point. Research focus has generally been placed on the cognitive, affective, and personality variables influencing the behavioral productions of individuals as they go about transmitting information to others, and, in turn, receiving information from others. Social context, when it is employed analytically at all, is generally considered a "thing" that surrounds the interactants; the latter are judged to possess intentions and traits of their own which can be separated from context. Thus, it is the individual as an independent transmitting and receiving entity which is the object of study.

This book questions whether communication can be studied adequately in this fashion, and so argues instead for the study of communication as a social process. It suggests that the starting point for communication analysis must always be the social group, rather than individual "senders" and "receivers." It is noteworthy, however, that this suggestion is not intended to establish a duality between people and society, or between subjective and objective worlds.

According to the argument in this book, the individual is not separate from society, but he/she is also not the initiator (or creator or sender) of either society or communication. Rather, social communication argues for an examination of persons as continuous social products, as entities ("moments") that are inextricably rooted in the ongoing processes and structures of the social group. Thus, the organization and function of communication viewed as a societal activity is the overarching concern of social communication and this book.

In writing this book, my goal has been to provide both a statement that summarizes and extends previous theoretical work on social communication and an articulation of selected methodological principles consistent with this statement. Although a number of research studies I have conducted or supervised are described, the emphasis is on exemplification and clarification of basic theoretical points, rather than on data analysis or presentation.

A number of questions are broached in this fashion: What does it mean to say that communication is a socially patterned, rule-governed process? What contextual boundaries are most productive in the study of face-to-face interaction? What is the relationship between the "micro" behaviors that communicators produce and contribute to social events and "macro" processes constitutive of society?

Answers to these questions should be of relevance to students of interpersonal relations, organizational dynamics, face-to-face interaction, conversational behavior, and the like. Indeed, I hope that one consequence of this book for readers will be an awareness that the study of institutional and organizational communication is not separate from interpersonal communication, and that discourse research and nonverbal analysis are central, not peripheral, to the study of interpersonal relations. My position here is that the notion of behavioral codes—multilevel, hierarchical structures of behavior—can be used as a unifying theme.

Although this book is concerned with a social approach to communicative interaction, the present argument is significantly different from the local construction orientations of some ethnomethodology and conversation analysis. Social communication theory recognizes that such basic societal categories as gender and class are constructions that are accomplished through interaction. Yet social communication, as I understand it and articulate it here, does not see the social world as created de novo each time interactants come into each other's presence. There is a historical continuity to the patterns of social life; these patterns are constituted by hierarchical structures that transcend single face-to-face moments, and are not well formulated by views of the world as locally managed and lived. Moreover, the differential nature of persons' access to particular communication resources—including here everything from ownership of a television to command over "standard" pronunciation—also requires a structural view of society. True, status differences between and among participants are not a priori, static objects, but are developed and established during the moment-by-moment unfolding of interactional events; yet the particular behaviors that actors contribute to interaction are highly regulated and are drawn from limited repertoires of behavior. What may appear to the individuals as the working out and creation of social structural differences (or similarities) may appear from a "higher" analytic level to constitute the invocation, (re)production, and continuation of historically based behavioral forms and patterns.

Acknowledgments

A number of colleagues were kind enough to read and respond to various portions of the manuscript for this book. I appreciate the advice (and encouragement) of Robert Hopper, Wendy Leeds-Hurwitz, Madeleine Mathiot, Charles Petrie, Marvin Scott, Sari Thomas, and Yves Winkin. The participants in my spring 1986 graduate course, Seminar in Interpersonal Communication, were both helpful and patient as I initially worked out some of these ideas in lecture and on the board. Three advanced graduate students in social communication, William Morphis, Sheila Sullivan, and Marcley Wendell, met with me on a regular basis to fine-tune my conceptualization and articulation. Jo-Anne Levy's current dissertation work, originally begun independently of this book, encouraged me to believe that the various conceptual distinctions drawn here could be usefully applied to ethnographic data. Joan Ford was temporarily willing to leave the world of literary criticism to help edit some of the manuscript's social science jargon (of which, alas, much remains). Peter Emmerich's assistance with entering the bibliography into the computer freed me to do other chores. To all these folks, a hearty thanks is due.

The Julian Park Publication Fund, of the State University of New York at Buffalo, helped defray some costs in the preparation of the book. In general, the resources made available to me by the university are to be commended and are certainly appreciated.

Two intellectual debts are also in order. My understanding of social communication theory initially derives from my studies with Ray L. Birdwhistell at the University of Pennsylvania; Birdwhistell's scholarly rigor and creativity set the standards. The late Erving Goffman kindly opened his home to me on several occasions to discuss a variety of matters; he once predicted that I would one day write something akin to what now appears as chapter 3.

I am grateful to the following for permission to reprint portions of copyrighted material:

The American Sociological Association and Prof. Gillian Sankoff, for permission to quote from: E. Goffman. "The Interaction Order," *American Sociological Review,* vol. 48 (1983), 1–17.

Lorraine V. Aragon, for permission to quote from: L.V. Aragon. "Topics of Conversation: A Study of Patterns in Social Discourse," unpublished M.A. thesis, University of Pennsylvania, 1978.

Prof. Ray L. Birdwhistell, for permission to quote from: R.L. Birdwhistell. *Introduction to Kinesics.* Washington, D.C.: Foreign Service Institute, 1952.

Cambridge University Press, for permission to quote from: K.R. Scherer and P. Ekman (eds.). *Handbook of Methods in Nonverbal Behavior Research.* Cambridge: Cambridge University Press, 1982.

Gordon and Breach Science Publishers, for permission to quote from: S.C. Heilman. "Communication and Interaction: A Parallel in the Theoretical Outlooks of Erving Goffman and Ray Birdwhistell," *Communication,* vol. 4 (1979), 221–234.

Prof. Sally Jackson, for permission to quote from: S.A. Jackson. "Speech Acts as the Basis for Conversational Coherence." Paper presented to the Speech Communication Association, Washington, D.C., 1983.

Mouton de Gruyter and Prof. Dean MacCannell, for permission to quote from: D. MacCannell. "Commemorative Essay: Erving Goffman (1922–1982)," *Semiotica,* vol. 45 (1983), 1–33.

Sage Publications, for permission to quote from: R.T. Craig and K. Tracy (eds.). *Conversational Coherence: Form, Structure, and Strategy.* Beverly Hills, Calif.: Sage, 1983.

Sage Publications, for permission to quote from: L.L. Putnam and M.E. Pacanowsky (eds.). *Communication and Organizations: An Interpretive Approach.* Beverly Hills, Calif.: Sage, 1983.

Prof. Gillian Sankoff, for permission to quote from: E. Goffman. Unpublished lecture, Department of Anthropology, University of Pennsylvania, 1979.

Springer-Verlag, for permission to quote from: K.J. Gergen and K.E. Davis (eds.). *The Social Construction of the Person.* New York: Springer-Verlag, 1985.

Prof. Karen Tracy, for permission to quote from: K. Tracy. "The Issue-Event Distinction: A Rule of Conversation and Its Scope Conditions." Paper presented to the International Communication Association, Los Angeles, 1982.

University of California Press, for permission to quote from: A. Giddens. *The Constitution of Society.* Berkeley: University of California Press, 1984.

University of Chicago Press, for permission to quote from: E. Goffman. "Felicity's Condition," *American Journal of Sociology,* vol. 89 (1983), 1–53.

University of Chicago Press, for permission to quote from: V. Turner. "Social Dramas and Stories about Them," *Critical Inquiry,* vol. 7 (1980), 141–168.

University of Chicago Press and Prof. Walter Goldschmidt, for permission to quote from: W. Goldschmidt. "An Ethnography of Encounters: A Methodology for the Enquiry into the Relation between the Individual and Society," *Current Anthropology*, vol. 13 (1972), 59–78.

University of Chicago Press and Prof. Lawrence Rosen, for permission to quote from: L. Rosen. *Bargaining for Reality: The Construction of Social Relations in a Muslim Community*. Chicago: University of Chicago Press, 1984.

University of Chicago Press and Prof. Eviatar Zerubavel, for permission to quote from: E. Zerubavel. *Patterns of Time in Hospital Life: A Sociological Perspective*. Chicago: University of Chicago Press, 1979.

University of Pennsylvania Press, for permission to quote from: R.L. Birdwhistell. *Kinesics and Context*. Philadelphia: University of Pennsylvania Press, 1970.

Finally, the usual disclaimer: While I appreciate the insights and critical readings offered by several people, I admit that I have stubbornly stuck to my ideas and phrasings in places too numerous to mention. I alone bear responsibility for the final version.

A Perspective on
Social Communication

1
Social Communication Theory

This chapter presents an initial description of social communication theory. It begins by questioning some of the underlying assumptions of psychological orientations to communication, and then proposes the utility of sociocultural orientations in their place. The relevance of social communication theory to the study of everyday face-to-face interaction is a highlighted theme.

Over the last decade, the discipline of communication has developed an interest in the examination of interaction as a form of structured social action. Such recent communication research focuses on conversation as "an activity which should itself be a topic for research" (Nofsinger, 1977:12), and on behavior as a sort of "technology" (Hopper, 1983) facilitating the construction of interactional events. Studies operating within this framework emphasize the rules that make the orderly and meaningful exchange of information possible. Pearce writes, "The function of naturalistic study of conversation is to explicate actors' meanings for the brute facts of conversation, and, in my judgment, best proceeds by identifying the sets of rules which govern and guide the production and interpretation of messages" (1977:53). The results of this research program are impressive, covering such topics inter alia as speakers' construction of discourse coherence (Craig and Tracy, 1983); arguments (Jackson and Jacobs, 1980); turn-taking units (Nofsinger, 1975; Wiemann and Knapp, 1975); and accounts (McLaughlin, Cody, and Rosenstein, 1983; Buttny, 1985).

Despite this research productivity, there are limitations imposed by rules analyses of interaction as currently practiced. First, the discipline has yet to take seriously the axiom that communication occurs through several simultaneous channels. There is little research on the *integrated multiple codes* that guide actors' verbal and nonverbal contributions to particular scenes or contexts (cf. Leeds-Hurwitz, 1986). Second, the significance of particular rules for the creation and maintenance of participants' social relationships has not been consistently or systematically addressed (see Sigman, 1983a). In a similar vein, Thompson critiques the ethnomethodological study of conversation, which has been influential in our discipline, for its failure "to explore the ways in which the analysis of language can be integrated with the study of the institutional and structural dimensions of social life" (1984:100). Most conversation and interaction analyses approach behavioral data from within the discourse "texts" produced by speakers during bounded face-to-face encounters (see Sigman, Sullivan, and Wendell, in press). Rarely do such analyses consider constraints imposed by the overarching social situation, the institutional context and multiepisode history of interaction, or the constitutive social positions and relationships. Behavioral coding operates on numerous levels (cf. Pike, 1967; Halliday, 1978), yet the multiple constraints on, and functions of, communication have not been systematic objects of research.

The present book is concerned with an approach to the study of communication—variously called the structural, the social, and the organic approach—which recognizes and is sympathetic to the above concerns. My aim is to articulate this perspective on the multiple patterns and functions of interactional behavior, and to indicate its utility in the study of a variety of social settings and activities. The conceptual framework outlined here is adumbrated in the work of Bateson (1972, 1980; Ruesch and Bateson, 1951); Birdwhistell (1970); Goffman (1959, 1971); Gumperz (1982); Hymes (1974); Kendon (1977); Pike (1967); Scheflen (1968, 1973, 1974); and others. Although diverging themes are certainly discernible in these works, there is also an integrated core concerned with communication that derives from linguistic, sociological, and anthropological theory and methodology.

This chapter proceeds first by considering the differences between individual and social approaches to the study of communication and then by detailing key features of social communication theory.

Two Approaches to Communication Theory

In an important historical and critical paper, Thomas (1980) assesses the current status of communication scholarship by describing two basic disciplinary paradigms: (1) the mechanical model, and (2) the organic model. Thomas points out that it is the former model which dominates contemporary thinking about communication; with a few notable exceptions (for example, Birdwhistell, 1970; Thayer, 1972), the latter model has yet to receive forceful articulation or concentrated scholarly attention.

The mechanical model is an activity-oriented one; it conceives of communication as "something done to somebody" (Thomas, 1980:437). It is also a person-centered model in that the individual interactants in a face-to-face encounter are seen as the initiation and termination points for communication. Whether depicted by a linear stimulus-response chain (Shannon and Weaver, 1949) or by a more complex diagram (Westley and MacLean, 1957), the mechanical model essentially portrays individual entities ("communicators") acting or impinging on each other. This is similar to the expressional model delineated—and ultimately critiqued—by Scheflen: "In taking such a view, the observer imagines the participant as (1) a subject who is expressing something or (2) as an object who is perceiving something and reacting to it as a response" (1979:3).

Applications of the mechanical model can be found in such research areas as interpersonal persuasion, communication deficits (for example, communication apprehension), and, as suggested above, even the more recent discourse studies (see the research papers in the journals *Communication Quarterly* and *Human Communication Research* over the last ten years). This model emphasizes "newness" and "change" with regard to information transmission. There is an emphasis on talk, and, moreover, on talk "getting across," that is, on communication that is successful.[1] According to the mechanical model, "behaviour is just behaviour, but communication occurs when new, potentially change-producing input is entered into the transmitting system" (Thomas, 1980:434).

The paradigm with which Thomas contrasts the mechanical model is labeled the "organic model." The organic model derives from an "alignment with disciplines traditionally associated with the study of social system and structure . . . , rather [than] with the area known as 'speech' (and sometimes extended to 'speech communication')" (1980:437). The term *organic* is intended to signal the importance of the societal context of communication, rather than the mechanics of linear information transmission. Thomas's paper does not devote much space to the organic model, and, as this is the approach assumed in the present book, I will use the remainder of this chapter to delineate some of the basic propositions.

My understanding of the organic model of communication is derived primarily from the published work of Birdwhistell (1952, 1970) and Scheflen (1965a, 1968, 1973, 1979). This material is, in turn, based on and/or congruent with selected aspects of a variety of sociological (Durkheim, 1933, 1938; Mead, 1934; Goffman, 1959, 1971), anthropological (Radcliffe-Brown, 1958, 1965; Bateson, 1972, 1980), and linguistic (Trager and Smith, 1951; Hockett, 1958; Pike, 1967; Hymes, 1974; Gumperz, 1982) insights. The following themes may be thought of as defining features of the organic approach to communication:

1. Take the social group (social system) as the unit of analysis, rather than individual psychological entities. In this regard, note that the communication system is responsive to, and is a dynamic part of, the social division of labor. (See Poole, Seibold, and McPhee [1985] for a similar starting point.)

2. Search for the hierarchical organization of behavior, and do not separate "behavior" and "context." Recognize that an analytic unit at one level of the hierarchical structure may be context for some other unit at a different level (cf. Piaget, 1970).

3. Consider communication as a continuous process; although it consists of apparently discrete or intermittent signals displayed over multiple channels, communication from the perspective of the total system is ongoing.

4. Recognize that communication is multifunctional, involving both new informational and integrational transmissions (Birdwhistell, 1952). Analyze the multiple functions of, and the multiple constraints on, group members' behavioral production.

5. Account for the socioculturally structured and defined "programs" and "codes" for members' behavior; attribute patterning and/or idiosyncracy only after first detailing in this fashion the numerous structural levels.

According to the organic model, "communication" refers to the continuous process of information flow within a social system.[2] Group members participate in this process by contributing appropriate behavior at appropriate moments, but the individuals themselves and particular face-to-face engagements do not represent the limits of, or the initiation and termination points for, communication.[3] As socially delimited information flow, communication is organized and has a historical continuity beyond the life or behavioral contributions of any individual society member.

The five interrelated propositions are elaborated upon in the course of the discussion in the following section.

Social Communication

Golding and Murdock (1978) suggest that no theory of communication can be forthcoming without a commensurate theory of society and of the place of communication processes in society. Birdwhistell similarly writes, "Research on human communication as a systematic and structured organization could not be initiated until we had some idea about the organization of society itself" (1970:72). The organic approach to communication takes as its starting point society as an "objective facticity" (Berger, 1963), as an analytic abstraction as real as any other utilized by science (Lundberg, 1939; Mandelbaum, 1973). In Durkheim's (1938) words, society is an entity sui generis, and the behavioral performances of society members are conditioned by regularities that exist at the social level (O'Neill [1973] provides essays on the converse position, methodological individualism). This social level is supraindividual and multi-generational, comprising a history and pattern of behavior transcending any individual's biography, yet organizing and integrating the behavior of society members (cf. Kroeber, 1963).

Social communication theory, which is the particular variant of the organic model to be developed in this book (for an alternative, see Watzlawick, Beavin, and Jackson [1967], is based in part on considerations of society as both a structural entity and a supraindividual behavioral process. Communication in this view is seen not as an individual-level phenomenon, but as a societal-level one. More specifically, communication is conceived of as a process that functions to integrate and support the diverse components of society (or of selected subgroups), of which separate actors are but one of many. Birdwhistell (1970) defines communication as the dynamic or processual aspect of social structure, and as that behavioral organization which facilitates orderly multisensorial interaction. Scheflen similarly writes, "Communication can be defined . . . as the integrated system of behavior that mediates, regulates, sustains and makes possible human relationships. We can, therefore, think of communication as the mechanism of social organization." (1965b:26). Communication is considered to be a means by which the biosocial interdependencies of species members are maintained (cf. Lundberg, 1939; LaBarre, 1954), and a means by which their behavior is predictably ordered.

Social communication theory suggests that communication not be reductively defined as a process through which individual cognitions are exchanged, or as a process of information transmission between isolates (for example, "senders" and "receivers"). While it is certainly the case that individuals transmit messages to others about internal states and often do so intentionally, it is suggested that interpersonal (or interindividual) messages do not typify or exhaust the human capacity and the group requirement for communication. Pittenger, Hockett, and Danehy write in this regard:

> It is not really useful to think of individuals as the units out of which groups and societies are constructed; it is more fruitful to think of an individual [or the dyad] as the limiting case of a group when, for the moment, there is no one else around. It is treacherously misleading to think of language and other communication systems as cloaks donned by the ego when it ventures into the interpersonal world: rather, we think of ego (or "mind") as arising from the internalization of interpersonal communicative processes. (1960:223)

Just as individual persons are moments in society, so interpersonal behavior is a moment in social communication.

Communication thus appears as a concomitant of all social life and as an exigency of social survival in general, not primarily as a consequence of either individual motivation or initiative. Indeed, from a social communication perspective, motivation and initiative are socially programmed features of mind, that is, delimited options for the appearance of consciousness, emotional display, and verbal reference to consciousness and conduct (cf. Blum and McHugh, 1971; Hochschild, 1983; Denzin, 1984). For example, Heritage and Watson's (1979) analysis of one structural element of conversation, namely, "formulations," demonstrates that personality attributions or assessments require an understanding not of the presumed "internal" workings of people but of *standard and nonstandard courses of action* available to society members.

"Humorless," "unsympathetic," "hostile," and so forth are evidenced in interactants' adherence and nonadherence to specific sequential relationships between and among behavior units. Personalities do not "cause" persons to act in certain ways; certain ways of acting provide materials for the construction of social identities and are subject to social regulation and definition. Goffman's focus on the behavior of interaction is influential here: "I assume that the proper study of interaction is not the individual and his psychology, but rather the syntactical relations among the acts of different persons mutually present to one another" (1967:2). In other words, emphasis is placed on the organizing patterns (rules) of behavior and not on traits of persons.

It follows from this discussion that communication can be defined as a process of information handling—including activities of production, dissemination, reception, and storage—within a social system (cf. Wilden, 1979). This process provides for members' behavioral predictability and ensures societal (group) continuity. Communication is the means by which social reality is created, lived through, sustained, and/or altered. Rather than a process whereby information about an external, "real" world is shared *by* individuals, it is the mechanism whereby information is used to construct reality *for* individuals (cf. Berger and Luckmann, 1967; Carey, 1975; Pearce and Cronen, 1980). As implied above, it also serves to constitute group membership, to create the social boundaries of persons. Communication establishes meaningful distinctions between and among persons, objects, and behaviors, and defines the structure and goals of interactional events. In this sense, communication is the active or dynamic aspect of social reality, although this does not mean that all persons having membership in a group share identical vantage points on social reality. Rather, as described in greater detail below, there is a supraindividual patterning to the related yet separate social realities, for example, knowledge states and communication rules, which group members are permitted to access. Thus, the suggestion that communication and social reality are related is not intended to mean that individuals, at particular moments of interaction, *construct* or *create* social reality. Instead, social communication proposes that interactants' behavior serves to *recreate* and *invoke* the historically prior and continuing social reality (cf. McCall and Simmons, 1978).

Communication involves a dynamic structure that allows or prohibits various orders of information or message flow.[4] Research emphasis within social communication is directed toward the continuities and regularities of this information flow over time, rather than toward discrete transmission moments. Focus is placed on the socially constructed limitations or rules governing message flow, and on the functioning of these limitations for the social group under consideration.[5] In this manner, the traditional disciplinary concern for speaker/hearers' message production and reception abilities—that is, "output" and "input" trait variables—gives way to analyses of the semiotic codes and the social contexts that sustain *continuous* information flow within society.

Communication defines and organizes the spatiotemporal features of interactional events; the sensorial contact among persons "forcing" either focused or unfocused behavior (Goffman, 1963); the membership and behavioral requirements sustaining each interactional event; and so on.

It is in the sense of communication as a continuous social phenomenon that the two axioms "one cannot not communicate" (Waltzlawick, Beavin, and Jackson, 1967) and "nothing never happens" (Smith and Trager, cited by Pittenger, Hockett, and Danehy, 1960:234) take on meaning. The social environment is in a constant state of messagefulness, although selected channels and participants may be momentarily "silent." Communication as a totality takes place and endures even though certain channels are not actively employed at particular moments. Moreover, one cannot not communicate because one indeed does not communicate; rather, *one partially contributes behavior to the supraindividual process of communication.*

It should be stressed that by postulating communication as a social process, organic communication theorists do not intend for the word *social* to imply simply individuals in association, in collectivities, in the physical and interactional copresence of others. Rather, communication processes are considered *societal* phenomena, prerequisites for the continuity, integration, and adaptation of a social system. This social system comprises interdependent members and patterns of behavior that transcend the individual (Durkheim, 1933, 1938; Linton, 1936, 1940; Kroeber, 1963; Radcliffe-Brown, 1965; Sorokin, 1947).

For example, communication serves to articulate and sustain the processual aspects of the social division of labor. This division of labor functions to allocate responsibility for the group's process and to integrate the diverse activities constitutive of the social group. Individual contributions to the division of labor are not necessarily identical or equivalent. Aberle and his colleagues write of the significance of communication for the division of social labor thus: "Communication is indispensable if socialization and role differentiation are to function effectively" (Aberle et al., 1950:106). Kemper similarly notes, "If actors are engaged in coaction to complete a task, there is inevitably communication between them. . . . Thus, the arrangement of actors in the division of labor coincides in an important sense with the pattern of communication between them" (1972:743). The behavior displayed in particular interactional episodes draws upon codes, or integrated sets of rules, which enable the participants to signal (1) their places in the social hierarchy; (2) the amount and type of work responsibility they may be expected to contribute to various activities and contexts; and (3) the integration of their behavior with that found in other episodes and on the part of other group members. Joos describes one set of such signals for recruiting persons on behalf of the division of labor as follows:

The community's survival depends on cooperation; and adequate cooperation depends on recognizing the more and less responsible types of persons around us.

> We need to identify the natural burden-bearers of the community so that we can give them the responsibility which is heaviest of all: we make them responsible for cooperation itself. (1967:14–15)

Individuals contribute unequally and incompletely to the behavior that is constitutive of particular interactional scenes and events. Reciprocally, there is a differential distribution of rules and resources for conduct across societal members (see Poole and McPhee, 1983).

Communication is not a single, temporally linear process; a number of subsidiary processes, temporal laminates, and behavioral consequences can be discerned. For example, Erickson and Shultz (1982) recognize two aspects of the social organization of time: *kairos*, the appropriate or right time for a particular action; and *chronos*, the duration of an activity that is mechanically measurable via clock time. Both orders of time contribute to the regulation and structuring of communication.

The multilevel organization of communication can also be seen in terms of multiple message functions. Birdwhistell, for example, distinguishes two dynamic features of messages, which he labels "integrational" and "new informational" communication:

> "Integrational" communication involves such interaction as invokes common past experiences and is related to the initiation, maintenance or severance of interaction. "New informational," while symbolically consistent with and made up of past experience, involves the inclusion of information not held in common by the communicants. (1952:3–4)

In a more recent formulation, Birdwhistell (1970) extends the notion of integrational communication processes to comprise regulation of interaction, maintenance of systemic operations, and cross-referencing of particular message units to those contexts providing for their comprehensibility (see also Scheflen, 1968; and chapter 5). Lasswell suggests the recognition of three functional processes (see also Jakobson [1960] and Halliday [1978]):

> Our analysis of communication will deal with the specializations that carry on certain functions, of which the following may be clearly distinguished: (1) the surveillance of the environment; (2) the correlation of the parts of society in responding to the environment; (3) the transmission of the social heritage from one generation to the next. (1971:85)

Of special note here is the idea that communication serves multiple social and interactional ends and that a given unit of behavior can be seen to fulfill several such functions. In addition, there is an awareness of, and an emphasis on, messages of system stability, continuity, monitoring, and/or adaptation, rather than on those associated solely with person change. (As an example, chapter 4 is concerned with the interactions constituting a social group's recruitment procedures.)

The social communication position calling for studies of messages of continuity and predictability is designed to contrast with the mechanical model's
apparent emphasis (or overemphasis) on novel information transmissions
(Thomas, 1980). I have elsewhere written that within contemporary discourse
and interaction analysis, the mechanical approach fails to account for the many
messages (or message units) which seemingly function to signal the development, stability, and continuity of the participants' social relationships and group
affiliations (Sigman, 1983a). Moreover, I suggest that the examination of the
verbalizations exchanged within a single interactional episode for some "internal" organizing principle essentially precludes consideration of the *continuities
of information across episodes* that form the full pattern of the social information system. In this respect, chapter 2 considers discourse repetitions across
episodes and the importance of accounting for their functioning in both social
and interactional terms.

It should be noted that from a social system perspective, a behavioral function is not always, nor necessarily, seen as isomorphic with an actor's intentions for producing a particular unit of behavior (see Radcliffe-Brown, 1965;
Merton, 1968; Scheflen, 1973; Sigman, 1980a; Giddens, 1984). The usefulness
of a distinction between group-level and individual-level (psychological) functions when studying face-to-face interaction is summarized in the following:

> We need not explain the regularities observed in social interaction by reverting
> to the interests or motives of the individual. Instead, the system of interaction
> can be treated as having a structure of its own, sui generis. . . . Moreover, the
> structure of the interaction that results may bear little relationship to the motives
> with which persons entered the situation. (Aldrich, 1972:171)

In contrast, many definitions of communication explicitly concern themselves with intentional message transmission (cf. Fisher, 1978; Scott, 1977)
or delimit that part of social behavior which is communicative on the basis
of presumed intentions (cf. Cushman, 1980). Nevertheless, from the social communication perspective outlined above, an actor's ostensible motive for performing a particular behavior does not exhaust the regularity of that behavior
or the richness of its contribution to an interactional event and to the social
system at large. Although intentionality as a component of some communicative
activity cannot be denied, communication analysts should not be limited to
this aspect of behavior. Kockelmans writes that there is a legitimate "distinction between the meaning a phenomenon has for a society and the meaning
the same phenomenon may have for a particular individual who finds himself
in this or that particular situation" (1975:76).

That particular groups define communication in terms of actor intentionality, or differentially judge behavior as either intentionally or unintention-
ally performed, is not the same issue as suggesting that the communication
theorist examine all examples of socially patterned behavior. A distinction can
be drawn in this manner between a general and a culture-specific definition of

communication, between a broad social-scientific approach to the study of communication and a narrower native-delimited conception of what does and does not count as communication. Behavior for which individuals have intentions, that is, for which socially regulated and defined intentions are available and accountable, is not to be accorded different status for research purposes from that behavior for which no ostensible (verbalizable) intentions are forthcoming. The ranges of acceptable and unacceptable intentions for behavior are worthy of systematic study (cf. Gergen, 1982; Harré, Clarke, and DeCarlo, 1985).

Thus, this position does not deny or overlook social actors' possession and use of knowledge regarding their conduct and its spatiotemporal location (see Giddens, 1984), but it does situate such knowledge as part of the group's larger system of communication. The very notions of motive, intentionality, individual responsibility, and so on must be seen as semiotic tokens in a more encompassing network of actions and meanings. In this regard, non-Western cultural data remind us that not all groups account for persons' acts in terms of internal psychological states. Rosen writes, for example:

> A person's inner state [in Morocco] is largely irrelevant to an account of events in the world: since motive and intent are discernible in words and deeds, there is no felt need to discuss a person's interior state directly. (1984:169)
>
> Narrative accounts—whether as conversational exposition, oral history, or popular storytelling—work on the assumption that no man acts without contexts; therefore to reveal a person in a variety of circumstances is to reveal him as a social person. (1984:171)

The more encompassing network of meanings, for example, the vocabularies of motives and the conditions under which persons are socially expected to be responsible for their behavior (see Gerth and Mills, 1953), is the proper domain of social communication investigations.

The above discussion should not be taken to mean that social communication theorists assume a unilateral correlation between a unit of behavior and its function. Rather, each functional aspect of the communication process is said to represent only a heuristic abstraction from the total stream of behavior; communication events and the constituent behavior "partials" (see below) may serve numerous functions. Social communication analysts observe such multifunctionality of behavior in at least three interrelated ways. First, communication behavior appears to be a hierarchically structured process (cf. Pike, 1967).[6] As such, the contribution or function of communication units on one level of structure may not be the same as on other levels. A unit's functioning may be apparent for some (or all) of the levels considered. As Pittenger, Hockett, and Danehy write, "In theory, the relative importance of a single small event can be assayed by observing how far its effects 'reverberate' up through more and more inclusive larger events of which it is a constituent" (1960:250).

Moreover, social behavior is so structured as to involve multiples of hierarchies, and hierarchically arranged hierarchies; the same unit of behavior may thus be part of, and function within, one or more hierarchies (see chapter 3).

A second aspect of multifunctionality concerns the idea that, as noted above, the function and meaning of behavior for individual participants may not be isomorphic with the function of behavior for the social group (or for particular subcomponents within a society or group). This again is a consideration of level, although it attends to the relationship among social actors, social systems, and their constitutive behavior, not to the hierarchical patterning of the behavior itself. A further consideration here is that the same behavior may have different consequences (and different message values) for individuals, depending upon where in the social group they occupy statuses. For example, I have previously discussed the different group membership requirements that nursing-home staff members and residents may have for an entering patient; the same behavior exhibited by a newcomer may be interpreted by one group as a sign of "health" and "alertness" while seen by others as a sign of "mental unfitness" and "disease," depending on their institutional location and perspective (Sigman, 1982; cf. Annandale, 1985).

Finally, multiple codes constrain the form and contextual placement of participants' behavior; each such code provides for a meaning or function component of the behavior (cf. Frentz and Farrell, 1976; Halliday, 1978), and possibly more than one. A simple metaphor may be useful in clarifying this point. A behavioral form in its processing may be thought of as passing through a series of filters or generators before it is finally produced (performed) by a social actor; each filter, representing a particular social-behavioral code, shapes the behavior according to its own specifications and in interaction with other codes. Interactional behavior may be assumed to be conditioned by inter alia phonological, morphological, discursive, and interpersonal regulative principles; the behavior so produced provides information derived from each one of these semiotic constraints (cf. Halliday, 1978). For example, an utterance such as a greeting—more specifically, the particular form a greeting takes at any one time—may be conditioned by rules for sound production (partially embedding a sociolinguistic message regarding the speaker's socioeconomic background, among other things); social politeness (potentially transmitting information about the speaker's attitude toward the recipient); lexical choice (potentially including information on the speaker's level of education); and so on. In this manner, the multiple codes enable a greeting to serve numerous functions in interaction.

The notion of multifunctionality can be related to the notion of behavior "partials" (cf. Birdwhistell, 1970; Wilden, 1979). Individuals only partially possess or evidence all the rules constraining the totality of socially patterned behavior that constitutes the communication system, and not all individuals share the identical or fully overlapping codes for conduct (see Hymes, 1974; Bernstein, 1975).[7] Interactional events are composed of members' rule-governed behavior, yet the behavior of any individual interactant is an incomplete contribution to these events (cf. Mead, 1934; Birdwhistell, 1970). Interactional events require multiparticipant coordination in much the same way that, for example, a formal dinner party is comprised of, and emerges from, the nonoverlapping rules and behavior units of the domestic, who knows to "serve from the left and take from the right," and the guest, who knows only to signal completion of one course and readiness for the next. In accordance with the division of labor theory noted above, group members must have available to them (1) behavior for signaling their knowledge states and places within the overall social system, and (2) routines for coordinating their behavior partials with those of their fellows.

Poole, Seibold, and McPhee write, "Structures cannot be reduced to 'cognitive maps' in individual actors' heads" (1985:77). Nwoye's (1985) discussion of courtship among the Igbo of Nigeria presents a good illustration of the relevance of the concept of structural partials to the ethnographic study of continuous social communication. In the African group studied by Nwoye, courtship is a family affair proceeding from the man's having asked for the girl's hand in marriage: "The young man is joined by his parents, his relatives, and friends who start treating and behaving toward the girl as his 'wife' " (1985: 188–189). As a communication event, courtship in this group is spread across numerous interactions and is constituted by the partial contributions of a number of individuals (see also Rosen, 1984). The construction of an individual's social identity is likewise illuminated by the concept of interaction partials: "Evidence of this possession [of a self] is thoroughly a product of joint ceremonial labor, the part expressed through the individual's demeanor being no more significant than the part conveyed by others through their deferential treatment toward him" (Goffman, 1967:85).

The notion of partials leads to the methodological proposition that the analytic boundaries of a unit of behavior be seen beyond any individual group member's body; a unit of communication behavior may be constituted by the separate yet related contributions of several members. As Scheflen remarks, "A unit is not necessarily performed by one individual. A given unit, usually performed by one person, may be performed by several interactants on some occasions: e.g., one speaker may start a statement, another finish it" (1965b:20). (See Heritage and Watson's [1979] discussion of the collaborations involved in formulations of conversational topics.) Similarly, behavior performed by an individual may serve as a partial contribution to a group-level function; forms by several individuals, which complement each other or are integrated with each other, may in combination serve this particular function more completely. Discourse units separated by space and time, that is, occurring in what the social actors consider to be discrete events, can still be judged to constitute a single, albeit complex, message unit (see Sigman, 1983a; also chapter 2). Birdwhistell (1970) suggests that a communication event may last as briefly as a phoneme or as long as a generation or two. Pearce and Cronen similarly write, "The patterns of human action that exist in a marriage, a formal organization, or a nation may be extremely complex and take years or generations to emerge" (1980:161). Leach (1976) notes the message relatedness of symbols separated by many years, for example, as in the case of veils of marriage and of widowhood.

In addition, certain of the partials contributed to the constitution of particular interactional events are only indirectly offered by persons then present in the scene. Rapoport's (1982) discussion of the semiotics of the built environment indicates the importance of various architectural and physical elements for the meaningful construction of interactional events. In such cases, it is reductionistic and simplistic to suggest that the individual architect is communicating *to* the actors, or that the environment is merely a surround ("context") for behavior; rather, the architect and his/her design can be better seen as meaningful, albeit partial, units of the total scene's structure and composition.

Finally, any one interactional moment is a partial of the larger continuous system of information flow; communication systems, as noted above, are continuous, even though the "active" and partial message displays of particular individuals may not be.

These observations have implications for the appropriate size of analytic units and the "ethnographic present" (time framework) selected by researchers for their analyses (see Birdwhistell, 1977). Rather than look at the separate behaviors of various interactants in terms of their apparent role as either "stimulus" or "response," social communication theory highlights the larger scene or event that is accomplished and contributed to by the behaviors. The behaviors of individual interactants can be seen as the partial constituents of communication episodes requiring varying degrees of integration and coordination in adherence to the event "programs" (Scheflen, 1968). When studying interactional events as units of communication constituted by the partial contributions of multiple participants—as in the Igbo case just described—there are several patterns to be explored. The social communication investigator considers (1) the complete array of behaviors constitutive of the event; (2) the assignment of persons, for example, through recruitment and/or self-selection, to the different phases and subsidiary behavior units of the event; (3) signals available to the participants for coordinating their contributions and indicating the progression of the event; and (4) differential outcomes and evaluations of repeated communication events, based on the varying assignments of persons to behavioral contributions.

Plan of the Book

In the previous section, I began the construction of a framework for a social approach to communication study. The remainder of this book makes use of and elaborates upon this research perspective.

To recapitulate, as used here, *communication* refers to the continuous process of information flow within a social group. As an interdisciplinary academic endeavor, social communication studies the sets of group-defined rules which are allocated and adhered to by social actors and which account for the various patterns of this information flow in specific groups. Research emphasis is placed on the rules that define and delimit group members' acceptable behavior in various social settings, and the consequences of the different rules for the group.

Chapter 2 is concerned with building a means for studying interactional behavior which is consistent with social communication theory. The general theme of the chapter is that conversational data, as one type of interaction, can be analyzed from the perspective of the information they provide the researcher about the rule-governed processes involved in participants' construction of their social relationships. The approach attempts to bridge current interest in discourse analysis and the traditional communication concern for interpersonal relationships. The argument is that discourse analysts must recognize the social structural, as opposed to purely interactional, constraints on and functions of behavior.

The difference between social and interactional investigations is the major concern of chapter 3. This chapter is based on Goffman's (1983a) discussion distinguishing an "interaction order" from the rest of social life. On the whole, Goffman's (1961a, 1961b, 1963, 1967, 1969, 1971, 1974) work can be seen as an attempt to cordon off interaction as a sociological phenomenon sui generis. Chapter 3 questions the isolation of a discrete interaction order, and proposes a way of considering this feature of social organization so as to account for the multifunctionality of behavior.

Chapter 4 considers the concept of rule invocation, and is concerned with the multichannel and multifunctional communication rules in institutional settings. The chapter derives from two parallel ethnographic studies I conducted in 1978 and 1980–1981 on geriatric institutionalization (see Sigman, 1982, 1984, 1985/86, 1986). The discussion centers on the organization of People's Home into distinct wards as it contrasted with an "open" ward policy at Sisters of Faith Home.[8] Ward structure is not discussed as an administrative or managerial issue but rather as a communicational one. The various residential sections held different meanings for the individuals who lived and worked in each institution. Included in the discussion is an analysis of friendship patterns, group membership rites, territorial allocations, and clothing as these were related to ward organization. When institutional members acted, they invoked a variety of rules with a variety of attendant meanings; the nature of this multichannel invocation process is discussed.

Chapter 4 also examines communication and predictability. It suggests that all social groups develop and comprise patterns of standard behavior, expect their members to adhere to these patterns, and sanction individuals whose behavior deviates too far from the standard range. Many aspects of face-to-face interaction episodes, then, can be seen to be predictable and routine. Much of communication is concerned with the transmission of signals that indicate that the system as a whole, or some subsidiary component, is still in operation. These messages of predictability serve as a background against which novel messages (for example, emergencies and new information) come to be perceived and to take on meaning. Thus, chapter 4 is concerned with the various ways interactants can be seen to have and to rely on established patterns of predictable behavior, and to monitor cointeractants' behavior in order for this predictability to be upheld. Predictability is not seen as a fixed or given state, but rather as a process requiring semiotic tools for constant construction.

Although two nursing facilities serve as the basis for chapter 4, the discussion is centered around principles of social communication which are applicable to a range of interactional contexts. Each nursing home is described from the perspective of the continuous message flow that constituted it. A nursing home can be studied from a variety of perspectives: as a system of economic transactions; as an institution supplying health care to an elderly population; as a process and product of continuous multichannel communication; and so on. The third approach is taken here. As Hawes (1974) points out, rather than separate "communication" and "institution," so that communication *in* an institution is studied, the institution *as* communication becomes the object of investigation.[9] He writes:

> If we are to understand how social collectivities are created, maintained, and dissolved, we must infer from data the rules by which those social collectivities operate. . . . A social collectivity *is* patterned communicative behavior; communicative behavior does not occur *within* a network of relationships but *is* that network. (1974:500; emphasis in original)

From a social communication perspective, it is the multilevel information or message status of each institution which is discussed in chapter 4 (cf. Pacanowsky and O'Donnell-Trujillo, 1983). The application of this perspective to other interactional events and social institutions is also addressed.

Finally, chapter 5 provides a summary of the theory advanced throughout the book. The applicability of a social communication perspective to a variety of research questions is addressed in it, and a research agenda is noted.

Notes

1. See my earlier paper (Sigman, 1983a) for a review and critique of the conversation analysis bias toward studying new information and "deviations" from take-for-granted knowledge.

2. *Information* in this framework should be seen as "a difference which makes a difference" (Bateson, 1972), or as behavior that is meaningful. Information should not be thought of in its more technical sense, in which it is a numerical (probabilistic)

statement about behavior. Organic communication theorists specifically want to include predictable and repetitive information in their analyses and so disagree with Rapoport, who writes: "In *any* situation, information about something we already know is worthless as information" (1966:42; emphasis in original). In this regard, see chapter 2. Also, information is not to be understood as the "reduction of uncertainty" about an objective world. Information is the behavioral mechanism whereby the world is communicationally and socially constructed for, and made available to, persons. Information is thus a difference that makes a difference, as defined by a particular social group.

3. The economic system serves as a useful parallel. Any one business transaction must adhere to the patterns that constitute the system, and any one business transaction serves as a real-time instantiation of the system. Yet any one business transaction is but a moment of the more complete system.

4. The careful reader will have noted that I alternate between describing communication as a "process" and as a "structure." Communication is an *organized activity*, and can thus be studied from the two interrelated vantage points.

5. "Rule" is used in a most general sense to refer to statements about socially patterned procedures for behaving and interpreting (see Sigman [1980a]; Shimanoff [1980] for various uses of the term). Rules are analytic devices to account for behavior units; relations among behavior units; contextuality; and normative force (Sigman, 1985a). The degree of constraint that rules place on persons, and the definitions of the relevant interacting body or bodies, for example, persons, groups, and so on, to which rules apply are cross-culturally variable and are subject to empirical observation. Thus, social communication theory leaves open the possibility that normative and interpretive views of the social order and communication rules will be appropriate to varying degrees to different cultures (cf. Donohue, Cushman, and Nofsinger, 1980).

6. This is an axiom that guides certain structuralist methodologies (see Birdwhistell, 1970; Scheflen, 1973). For a limited criticism of this approach, see Condon (1980), who presents some data that question the total hierarchical organization of behavior. Note also that the guiding principle of hierarchy does not directly address the issue of whether a top-down or bottom-up view is most appropriate (cf. Scheflen, 1973; Kendon, 1982), that is, whether the hierarchy is seen as an organization of frame levels that constrain the appearance of behavior units on lower levels or as a structure built up from lower units. See chapter 2.

7. The mechanical model often seems to assume a nonequivalence of the interactants as well, at least in terms of their information states. However, this model usually sees communication as bringing the participants' information states more in line with each other, as in the case of the sender sending information to an unknowledgeable receiver. See chapters 4 and 5 for an elaboration on the social communication suggestion that communication need not involve isomorphic rules guiding participants' behavior or isomorphic information states resulting from interaction.

8. Fictitious names for places and persons derived from my data are used throughout the book.

9. I use the concept of "institution" in the present context in its dual sense as "standardised modes of behavior, [which] constitute the machinery by which a social structure, a network of relations, maintains its existence and its continuity" (Radcliffe–Brown, 1965:200), and as a spatially bounded "social establishment" (Goffman, 1961a:3). In both cases, the emphasis is on the communication interactions constituting the institution.

2
Above and Below Perspectives on Interaction

his chapter attempts a further elaboration of social communication theory by discussing a recent research concern of interaction study—the analysis of conversational coherence. In keeping with the initial perspective outlined in chapter 1, it is argued here that the study of how interactants seem to achieve coherence during particular interactional moments should be subsumed under the study of the continuities and patterns of information exchanged by the conversational partners spanning multiple episodes. The notion of coherence is thus expanded to include the rules governing interepisode continuities and repetitions of information. This chapter further suggests that as an alternative to the microanalysis of how actors make conversation work, researchers should focus on the system of continuous conversation of which social relationships are constituted. I argue for a movement away from studies of the "technology of conversation" (Hopper, 1983:83) and toward research on the macrocontexts that structure, and are constituted by, the interactants' behavior and relationships.

Above and Below Perspectives

Initial Definitions

To begin, I offer two characterizations of the research concerned with conversational coherence; I believe these descriptions may also be applied to interactional and interpersonal communication analyses in general. The two perspectives are here labeled the *from-below* and the *from-above* vantage points. The former views coherence as a result of speakers' unit-by-unit adherence to discourse relevance constraints. This perspective assumes that the coherence or connectedness of a complete discourse text is created or built up from the systematic and ordered relations of the units, for example, the turns and moves, which constitute a particular interactional moment. From this view, coherence is largely a product of linear or sequential chains of discourse utterances and their various interrelations, and for researchers, requires an analysis of the constraints that individual utterances place on each other.

In contrast, when the analyst looks at discourse from-above, coherence can be said to be a quality or feature of a conversation as a whole, more precisely, of a conversational episode (or a history of conversational episodes). From this view, coherence is not built up from "lower" units—if one assumes the existence of a strict behavioral hierarchy (cf. Pike, 1967; Birdwhistell, 1970)—but is somehow imposed on the total interaction. An interactional event, then, is considered the minimal relevant unit for analysis. To study coherence from this perspective, one examines what gets "accomplished" in a given interaction, and the degree to which this result is congruent with inter alia (1) a prior or preestablished agenda for that interaction; (2) previous interactional episodes engaged in by the same participants, whose knowledge of this interaction history influences the scope, content, structure, and duration of subsequent encounters; and (3) continuous interaction networks and institutions of which the particular event is a partial unit (cf. Goldschmidt, 1972).

My use of the terms *from-below* and *from-above* derives from the writings of those communication scholars who view themselves as structuralists—for example, Birdwhistell (1970), Scheflen (1973), Kendon (1977)—and whose method was heavily influenced by descriptive linguistics (see Trager and Smith, 1951; Hockett, 1958). Implicit in the structuralists' claim for a hierarchical organization for behavior is the utility of a distinction between coming (or approaching) from-below, and coming from-above, when collecting and analyzing communication data. The former usually involves micro-transcriptions of what Goffman (1979) calls "small behaviors" in order to establish the hierarchy and the overall organization of those behavior units. The small behavior units that are studied usually derive from a single communication channel, for example, lexical, kinesic, proxemic. The from-above perspective, on the other hand, isolates a behavioral level or system and examines the composition of internal (component) units and the constraints on their relations and appearances governed by that superordinate level of the hierarchy. The units that are studied in this manner are usually taken from a variety of communication channels, with the emphasis placed on how multichannel units interact with each other and constitute the superordinate level, for example, event.

Kendon (1982) provides a clear discussion of the differences between the two approaches, although he does not label them as I have here (see also Zabor, 1978). Kendon uses the example of a classroom lecture to distinguish from-below and from-above analyses:

> If we examine the lecture plan, as we may if the lecture has been written out in advance, we may see that it has a hierarchical structure, in the sense that the lecture as a whole may be seen as being divisible into component parts, such as an introduction, a middle, and a conclusion, and that these component parts

may themselves be further divisible into subparts. . . . These low-level components, however, although they are essential for the carrying out of the lecture plan, do not constitute the plan, either in themselves or in their combinations. The plan is not built up out of combinations of low-level components. The analysis of the lecture plan, therefore, does not proceed from the analysis of the elementary components upward to the larger units. Rather, the larger units are established first and are seen as frames or brackets for the lower-level units. (Kendon, 1982:481)

(See Cicourel [1980a, 1980b] for his comparable discussion of "bottom up" and "top down" approaches to discourse analysis.)

In operational terms, a social communication researcher usually needs to alternate between the two perspectives during the same project, although more weight is likely to be given to one or the other at any one time. Coming from-below enables one to be reasonably exhaustive in detailing units of behavior, while coming from-above enables one to see the multiple "tracks" (Goffman, 1974), "systems" (Mathiot, 1983), hierarchies, contexts, and so on in which these units operate and which provide them with form and meaning.

The above and below perspectives on the "same" data base usually reveal complementary, although not always identical, analyses. A from-below perspective analyzes the ordering of units constitutive of a single hierarchy, whereas a from-above perspective is able to examine the overlappings and interrelations of multiple hierarchies and channels (compare, for example, the structural analyses of Birdwhistell [1970] and Scheflen [1973] in this regard). As suggested, from-below analyses focus on a limited set of behavior units derived from a single source, while from-above analyses are concerned with a functional entity, for example, an interactional activity or event, and examine the units across multiple channels contributing to this entity.

Thus, this discussion represents a description of two orientations or places from which research on communication rules can begin, and from which a conceptualization about the organization of face-to-face interaction in general can be attempted. The above and below characterizations are relative perspectives with which one enters or contacts the continuous and hierarchical stream of discourse for research purposes; they are not specific entry points, for example, specific levels of discourse behavior, with which one commences an investigation. It is important to emphasize that the communication stream is not easily divided into micro and macro units or structures, but rather is seen to comprise a number of hierarchically organized levels and multiple hierarchies (cf. Pearce and Cronen, 1980; Kersten, 1986). These hierarchies are not necessarily discrete entities, for they may intersect with each other and share behavior units.

An example of both perspectives in use can be found in the recent communication literature on speech acts. Jackson (1983) maintains that utterances must attend to the *goals* established by previous speech acts, and not simply to surface propositional content, in order to be heard as coherent. She writes, "The coherence of a series of utterances—a conversation—is to be found not in utterance-by-utterance linkages, but in how each utterance contributes to an underlying, goal-oriented, speech act structure" (1983:1). (Presumably this goal is contributed to by other behavior in addition to speech acts.) Jackson thus considers goals as *general or global organizing principles* of discourse. However, specific goals and the symbolic acts that accomplish them are analyzable either from-above or from-below, as either institutionally given or individually (sequentially) produced. Goals can be linked to a discourse episode as a whole or to the individual utterances that constitute an episode (see Jacobs and Jackson, 1983).

It should be admitted that not all social behavior can be illuminated by the two perspectives. Some forms of data require one or the other intervention. Zerubavel (1979) provides an interesting and clear case in this regard. His data are concerned with the temporal features of interaction in a hospital:

> What forced me to "construct" the global temporal structure of the hospital in a mosaiclike manner, namely, the fact that hospital staff, including the designers of coverage schedules, had only fragmentary perspectives on it, is of a highly theoretical significance to the understanding of the temporal division of labor in it. It should be added that this mosaiclike temporal order does not derive in any planned way from "above," but, rather, seems to emerge quite spontaneously from "below," that is, from the more "local" organizational levels of the hospital. (1979:66)

In the hospital Zerubavel studied, several principles for organizing time were in operation, often interacting and conflicting with each other, and they did not contribute to (nor were they themselves organized by) any single institution-wide principle. Thus, the hospital temporal structure needed to be approached by the researcher from-below and not from-above.

Relationship to Research on Global/Local Relevance

The distinction between the from-above and from-below starting points for the study of interaction may appear similar to Tracy's (1982, 1983; also see Van Dijk, 1979) discussion of global and local frameworks for discourse relevance. One immediate difference is that Tracy is concerned with a cognitively based set of rules that enable conversationalists to speak competently and coherently. The above and below perspectives, on the other hand, are heuristic devices; they may be of use to researchers in developing potential units for analysis, but no claims can be made for their status as either psychologically or interactionally real.

While Tracy's research makes an important contribution to discourse scholarship by not being tied to the sequential relations of verbal units, it is nevertheless still text- and episode-bound. In this respect, it is still largely a from-below type of analysis. Whereas the terms *above* and *below* are not intended here to refer to a fixed level or unit of discourse behavior, Tracy's analysis of the global framework does directly concern itself with the overriding themes apparent in particular conversational episodes. These claims require a deeper discussion of Tracy's research program.

Tracy defines the local framework as "make your remarks relate to the last thing your partner talked about" (1982:1). The global framework states that speakers should "make your remarks relate to the main point of your partner's talk" (1982:1). Thus, Tracy's work is concerned with structures of text, albeit not simply in terms of individual, connected (or unconnected) utterances. Her research indicates a preference for issue rather than event elaborations. That is, conversational extensions of the generalized topic or issue are judged to be more competent than extensions of the specific incident or event portrayed in preceding utterances.

The following dialogue, which I have reconstructed, indicates that speakers are indeed aware of the differences between the two relevance frameworks, and may move to complete the larger thought unit of a discourse espisode (see Beach [1983] for a comparable use of reconstructed discourse):

A: I had a book overdue at the library thirty days today.

B: Thirty days. Wow. Did they charge you?

A: Three dollars. It's three dollars, or thirty dollars for the whole book.

B: I got a notice from Atlantic Research University, I have several books out from their library.

A: And they're due.

B: They're due. I'm going to the conference in March, some of my former colleagues are going to be there.

A: Oh, that's nice.

B: Yeah. I've got a paper. Fred Jones put together a session and he asked me.

A: Well that's good, that certainly counts.

B: Not really, it's only a conference. I thought the committees only look at refereed journals, articles in journals.

A: No, it's part of scholarship. They look at presentations. They want to see about four.

B: I didn't know that.

A: Yeah. . . . So you're going to give them the books to take back for you to—

B: Yeah. I've got to call them and tell them.

Speaker A's last turn ("Yeah. . . . So you're going to give them . . .") refers not only to the topic of the immediately previous utterance ("I didn't know that [conference presentations are part of scholarship]"), but to a theme initiated by B several turns back ("some of my former colleagues are going to be there").

In other words, the connectedness (coherence) of this dialogue becomes apparent only when the analyst examines the text as a whole and the issues it raises, rather than sequentially related or adjacent individual turns at talk. It is important to note, however, that both issues and events are confined to particular interactional episodes in Tracy's (1982, 1983) research program.

Goldberg (1983) also discusses the differences between global and local models of discourse coherence, arguing against linear analyses of speech behavior (cf. Frentz and Farrell, 1976). She defines global relevance in the following way:

> Initially, it is the theme's generic macrostructure (i.e., the pattern of development intrinsic to a particular discourse type or genre) that is the salient cohesive device chaining one locution to the next. The actual structures found in the discourse are determined by lower-level, text-specific macrostructures. (1983:27)

Goldberg suggests that from the analyst's perspective, it is difficult to predict which macrostructural theme(s) will constrain discourse contributions to nonroutinized interaction. Moreover, the emergent quality of interaction can be seen in that each speaker's turn at talk may delimit and indicate a different macrostructure. While individual participants may encode/decode messages based on the "agenda" or "program" (cf. Scheflen, 1968; McCall and Simmons, 1978; Sigman, 1983a) they are adhering to, or assume their cointeractants are implementing, casual conversation as a whole may not have any a priori theme or structure guiding it. Goldberg suggests that an analysis based on the relations among individual "moves" (communicative actions) is most appropriate for studying discourse coherence. This would appear to constitute an integration of from-above and from-below analyses, although again within single-episode confines.

In summary, this section has been concerned with delineating two research perspectives on the organization of interaction, and with relating these approaches to current conversation scholarship. The discussion in the following sections represents an attempt to describe some research questions related to a from-above and a social communication perspective on coherence.

A From-Above Definition of Coherence

Research on the relationship between the local and global relevance constraints on discourse represents an exciting area that is just beginning to develop in the study of communication. It can be suggested, however, that there are additional ways to examine from-above the interconnections and coherence of discourse behavior. For example, there are very few studies that examine *the relations between and among units occurring within separate interactional episodes.* I am not referring here to the fact that events which occur in a first encounter establish background knowledge (Beach, 1983) or taken-for-granted information (Hopper, 1981) which can be used by participants when adhering to the cooperative principle and the conversational maxims (Grice, 1975) during a subsequent encounter. Rather, interactants can be observed making behavioral ties or connections across several interactional events for a variety of reasons beyond that of adherence to the cooperative principle.

The following illustration from an interview subject, who is participating in a study of mine currently under way on behavior in "intimate" relationships, demonstrates multichannel relations between multiple events and their constituent activities:

> I was seeing this man, and he told me once that the last person he dated was really unknowledgeable, unsophisticated, didn't even know what brie cheese is. Well, so the second time we got together, he came to my place, I cooked dinner. I had some vegetables and dip beforehand. And some wine and cheese. [*Smiles.*] Brie.

This example depicts the interactant reporting an attempt to connect to a previous discourse topic with a rather strategic (albeit transparent) end in mind. It illustrates the degree to which speaker/hearers may, in general, attend to the form and content of their cointeractants' speech—especially, it would seem, when extended future contact is likely, required, or desired—and may use this information in subsequent encounters. Attention can be seen to have been placed by the interviewee on both the organizing logics and the attendant meanings (for example, the boyfriend's connection of cheese, a former girlfriend, and sophistication) of her cointeractant's previous talk. Importantly, speaker/hearers appear to use such information not merely to adhere to discourse relevance constraints. The particular behavioral tie in the preceding example seems to have provided the participant with a vehicle for a desired self-presentation (Goffman, 1959).

This example also demonstrates the connections that may exist between verbal and nonverbal behavior (including domestic and personal objects [Csikszentmihalyi and Rochberg-Halton, 1981]) contained in separate interactional events. Nonlexically encoded information becomes a part of the information repository of a social relationship in a manner comparable to that for lexical behavior (see below), and may enter into future interactional situations and contexts in a variety of ways (cf. Kreckel, 1981). In general, there are likely to be continuities in the manner, type, and content of exchanged information as participants develop a history of extended, focused interaction with each other.

The brie example illustrates that participants' previous interactions provide them with a repertoire of events and ideas for future reference. It seems most probably true that the brie need only have been briefly mentioned (if at all) during the second encounter described in the quote, since the interactional history of the participants would have allowed for sufficient information necessary for comprehension. However, an important feature of this event which remains masked by an "adherence to quantity constraints" analysis is that relational and interactional history becomes a *continuous resource* for communicative messages. This historical resource may be directly drawn upon by the participants in their construction of messages, and may eventually come to represent a constraining or conditioning force within the context of all future message encodings/decodings. As discussed more fully below, information resources can be observed establishing expectations for the range of acceptable and unacceptable conversational topics; they lead to participants' awareness of their cointeractants' behavioral preferences; and they delimit and define a relationship's typical codes of conduct.

In this manner, conversational coherence can be seen to comprise a consistency of utterances—more generally, of communicative acts—and of information invoked within and across multiple interactional episodes. As Leach notes, "Events which are separated by a considerable interval of time may be part of the same message" (1976:27). An appropriate unit for coherence analysis, then, is not only the adjacency pair, the triplet, or the topic or theme of a conversation (for a review of the relevant literature, see Coulthard [1977] and Levinson [1983]), but also the social rules regarding information flow between and among relationship members, and within and across diverse discourse episodes. As MacCannell suggests, "Each [utterance] constitutes an opening of the conversational circle onto the wider world of affairs" (1983:28). The social communication approach to talk is concerned with conversational behavior in relationship to this wider social world, and suggests that each conversational episode is but a moment in a more inclusive pattern.

A second example can be offered here. Several years ago I conducted interviews for a research project concerned with pet/owner bonding and interaction (Sigman, 1983b; see also Katcher and Beck, 1983).[1] During my second meeting with Mrs. H., an elderly dog owner who had volunteered to be part of the study, a reference was made to the claim by one of Mrs. H.'s neighbors that her dog (the neighbor's) has no fleas. At that time, Mrs. H. also made reference to the fact that this information had been shared with me on a previous occasion, during our first interview session. Mrs. H. did not explicitly say, "Do you remember what I said about Mrs. Y.'s dog?" or some such thing. Instead, in the middle of our conversation about community social relationships, Mrs. H. said to me in a high-pitched, almost mocking voice (the same tone she had first used), "My dog doesn't have fleas." She and I immediately began to laugh, which I took as a signal that we shared a similar attitude toward Mrs. H.'s neighbor and that we both remembered the previous conversation and information. A level of coherence, in the sense of topic consistency and continuity, can be seen in this dialogue when the conversation is cross-referenced with, and is seen as a partial of, the total information flow of my conversational relationship with Mrs. H. This type of phenomenon has not yet become an object of systematic communication or discourse analysis. As indicated above, it is obvious that I believe we should study the constraints that evolving relationship definitions place (from-above) on discourse.

Coherence can be defined as a relationship between an interaction (and its constituent utterances) and an agenda for that particular type of communication event. When Kendon (1982) looks from-above at the plan for a lecture, he sees not individually constructed units but a set of organizing principles and behaviors that define the lecture as a whole. Similarly, there exist programs for a variety of communication events, that is, frameworks that "provide for [the] performance of standard, recognizable behavioral units" (Scheflen, 1968:46). Temporally adjacent utterances may adhere to Grice's (1975) conversational maxims yet not be heard as relevant or appropriate by the participants, who are adhering to a more general set of constraints for that interaction. Agendas or programs provide for the *relevance and suitability* of talk within a given episode and across episodes, and are oriented to by speaker/hearers for the significance and meaning of their multichannel contributions.

A similar although somewhat more limited claim is made by Nofsinger, who analyzes lawyer-and-witness talk in terms of the knowledge state the lawyer attempts to construct. Nofsinger's (1983) data on courtroom discourse indicate that there are certain overriding tactical goals and strategies that determine questioning initiated by lawyers, the responses by witnesses which are considered appropriate, and the full information during a trial which the judge and jury receive. Nofsinger suggests that, in contrast, the goal of most casual conversation is simply to keep talk going, and so he does not recognize the applicability of agendas to these occasions.

It should be stressed that agendas are not simply frameworks that constrain contributions to a particular interaction, akin to "macrostructures" and "global relevance" frameworks (cf. van Dijk, 1979; Tracy, 1982; Goldberg, 1983). Rather, the implementation of one agenda through the participants' selection from a repertoire of all possible agendas, and the actual content (the topic-related information) developed as part of the agenda implementation, are features that transcend any single interactional moment. That there is a continuity of interaction behavior across temporally discrete episodes is accounted for by the presence of a limited set of agendas or programs from which behavioral choices over time may be made.

As noted above, Tracy's (1982, 1983) research indicates that there is a speaker preference for issue rather than event elaborations, and that speakers are judged more competent if they adhere to the global as opposed to local coherence and relevance frameworks. Van Dijk (1983:33) similarly concludes, "To be meaningful, a discourse should not only be locally coherent, but also globally coherent—there must be some kind of 'semantic unity' to the whole discourse." While I do not suggest here that there is a preferential maneuvering (in the sense of frequency of occurrence) for interepisode coherence and for the type of agenda adherence described above, nevertheless I do consider that some of this can be interpreted in the dialogues of *continuous interactional partners*. The following section discusses a number of research avenues in this vein.

Discourse and Relationship Coherence

Once one takes a from-above perspective on discourse, it becomes necessary to study discourse events in their historical context, that is, discourse embedded in continuous social relationships and repetitive social encounters. This broad contextual knowledge should enable the researcher to understand the program-based constraints on discourse and the relationship between particular moments of interaction and the larger pattern(s) of information flow. This research approach is thus sensitive to the duality of patterning described by Giddens: "The opposition between 'micro' and 'macro' is best reconceptualized as concerning how interaction in contexts of co-presence is structurally implicated in systems of broad time-space distanciation—in other words, how such systems span large sectors of time-space" (1984:xxvi).

The preference expressed in this chapter for the from-above perspective reflects my belief that communication researchers need not, and perhaps should not, be as language- and text-centered as they currently are. Given previous disciplinary concerns for interpersonal relationships, it would seem that communication researchers have an opportunity to study interactional rules in a manner quite different from linguists, ordinary language philosophers, ethnomethodologists, and the like. My interest in the from-above perspective thus derives from a concern for, and a delineation of, a particular field of study within communication: *I believe we should study human relatedness, the various semiotic forms it takes, and the multiple functions of particular group-prescribed codes of behavior.* In this manner, the analysis of discourse coherence gives way to the study of relationship coherence, more specifically, the information coherence of social relationships. This orientation facilitates the study of the continuous information flow within and across particular interactional networks, contexts, and communities, which is a primary goal of social communication investigators. The remainder of this chapter discusses this combined analysis of discourse and relationship behavior.

Research Questions and Directions

The suggestion that conversational coherence can be studied from-above essentially directs communication analysts to a consideration of the *patterns of information flow that sustain particular social relationships and situations.* The goal of such analyses is to examine the types of information regularly shared (or not shared) by relationship comembers and interaction participants (see chapter 3 for a discussion of the implications of the various ways to label communicators), and the manner and contexts in which this information is handled.

As an alternative to the study of how actors make conversation work, researchers should focus on the system of *continuous conversation* in which social relationships are embedded. This emphasis represents a movement away from an analysis of the rules for discourse production and toward the patterns of relationship (re)construction via information coherence. That communicators can produce utterances that cohere with, or are relevant to, those of their fellows, is judged here to be secondary to the observation that participants' communicational relationships are characterized by a continuity and regularity of information exchange. The apparent coherence of selected discourse units is framed by the information continuities that exist at a societal level of analysis. A related point is made by Thayer, who advocates a social systems approach to communication theory:

> To look at two homogeneous members of a homogeneous epistemic community and to be interested in the fact that they can "communicate effectively" with one another on certain topics is to miss what is at issue almost entirely. They can do so because they have been "programmed" to be able to do so. . . . Homogeneous socialization is one source of the "effectiveness" of human communication, and we should look to the source and not to the "message" to see what is going on. (1972:118–119)

As Heilman notes in summarizing the contributions of Birdwhistell (1970) and Goffman (1959, 1961a, 1961b, 1967, 1974) to social communication theory, "What people choose to highlight or tell one another can no more be separated from the group-created cosmos of meaning than can what is grammatically permissible be separated from socio-cultural order" (1979:223). Thus, interactional episodes are to be studied as instances of more global and continuous systems of meaning and order.

Frentz and Farrell argue along similar lines against particularistic analyses: "It is only the encompassing form of an episode which allows for the meaningful explanation of more particularistic communicative acts" (1976:335). I would simply add that the apparently discrete episode need not be considered the limit of analysis, and that investigators should search for forms and patterns relating and extending across several interactional moments. Birdwhistell indicates that "each piece of experience (of whatever duration) exists in a larger context which structures its function in the communication system" (1970:16). Each interactional episode, viewed as unit rather than context, is a piece or moment of some larger episode, event, activity, or process.

The from-above goal for research does not preclude the study of coherence in terms of speakers' adherence to the cooperative principle (Grice, 1975), the given-new contract (Clark and Haviland, 1977), or the issue-event distinction (Tracy, 1982, 1983). However, it does pursue an investigatory course that recognizes the multiple constraints placed on discourse and the multiple social and interactional functions served by discourse. Adherence to the cooperative principle is itself considered to be subject to conversationalists' selection and thus capable of conveying a variety of interpersonal meanings. The present section discusses some of the existing research in this area, emphasizing the dual contribution this literature makes to an understanding of interactional structures and social relationship processes. There are three research areas to be explored here: (1) the strategic uses of relationship information; (2) the functioning of information continuities for the construction and maintenance of interpersonal relationships; and (3) the range of permissible topic formulations.

Strategy. The coherence or connectedness of discourse relative to the constraints described by Grice (1975) and others is concerned with the information held by interactants, and the degree to which this information can be relied upon by speakers and hearers for disambiguating, contextualizing, and interpreting utterances. Various authors refer to this information as "background under-standings" (Beach, 1983); as "taken for granted [TFG] information" (Hopper, 1981); as "intersubjectivity" (Rommetveit, 1974); and as "shared knowledge" (Kreckel, 1981). The underlying research framework suggests that in order for speakers to be in compliance with, for example, the maxim of quantity, it is necessary that they take background knowledge into account and say only what needs to be said, and no more. Potential interpretive ambiguities or errors are considered to be largely eliminated by the interactants' reliance on shared social and contextual knowledge. In a sense, information that can be taken for granted must be taken for granted by message encoders and decoders.

Analyses of interpersonal relationships and of strategic behavior render such a categorical assertion questionable. For example, there does not exist a one-to-one correspondence between the information that is held in common (or thought to be held in common) by discourse participants and the actual utilization of and reference to this information during specific face-to-face encounters. Goffman points out that background social knowledge, interactional and relational history, and current (here-and-now) circumstances do not so much provide for information that is "given" as they do information that is "recallable":

> A conversation builds up a fund of matters that can be referred to succinctly, providing one of the reasons why we are inclined to "fill in" a latecomer. The problem, then, is that one passes by degree from what can be taken to be in immediate consciousness to what can be more or less readily recalled thereto, the *given* changing gradually to the *recallable*. (Goffman, 1983b:13)

The shift from considering TFG as information that *must* be taken into account when generating discourse contributions, that is, by using it to warrant the brevity and incompleteness of particular utterances, to that which can and *may* be called into play is an important one. Within this revised analytic scheme, discourse is no longer constrained simply by relevance conditions but is instead responsive to a variety of strategic formats for message production. Sanders (1983:80) writes that it is "optional rather than obligatory to actively utilize cohering devices" and that we must treat coherence as a tool rather than as an obligation. There appears to be considerable latitude in discourse participants' construction and utilization of taken-for-granted information. In addition, discourse contributions can be seen to be subject to several conversational and relational constraints (cf. Butterworth, 1978).

When one studies conversation as an enduring social enterprise, as a process of symbolic interaction extending across numerous contexts and episodes by the same participants, research attention must be directed toward the rules that regulate and constitute the totality of information flow. In addition to considering information that can be taken for granted, conversational coherence studies must focus on the information that can, must, and/or must not be invoked (referred to) during particular interactions. As indicated above, information may be held in common by discourse participants, yet the relationship definition may require the speakers to act as if that information did not exist. An example is when George and Martha in Albee's (1962) *Who's Afraid of Virginia Woolf?* initially must not mention their imaginary son to their guests. Alternatively, speakers may act as if they have information in common even though they do not (Goffman, 1969; Handel, 1982), either in hopes that the information will eventually surface or that the relationship definition usually coincident with that information will be assumed by the other participant(s).[2]

Kreckel (1981) observes that not everything that is available for conversation is actually taken up, and not everything that is said is shared by the interactants. Moreover, "Everything connected with the speaker is a potential source of information for the addressee. However, different sources do not enjoy equal status with regard to their respective salience for the recipient" (1981:50). Although Kreckel's remarks are intended to refer to the differential salience of particular communication modalities, the same argument can be made for particular communication participants. In a series of observations I conducted in nursing institutions, for example, there were a number of cases in which nurses seemingly refused to search for possible TFG information in order to interpret certain patients' verbalizations "completely" (see Sigman, 1985b, 1986). Those patients who were considered by the staff to be "senile" were required to be explicit during conversation, not assume or rely on shared knowledge, and provide for all anaphoric referents. As Sanders (1983) indicates, interpreters (given their place and role in the social group) may decide to accord competence to cospeakers and attribute coherence and meaningfulness to their produced utterances, or they may decide against this. At the nursing home, there were predictable occasions when interactants acted as if conversational referents were not known, and avoided or delayed searching for suitable interpretive frameworks.

From a social communication perspective, the assumption that discourse participants always "take the role of the other" or share in the construction and utilization of an intersubjective state (cf. Mead, 1934; Rommetveit, 1974) must be questioned. Goffman writes in this regard:

> This assumption of full intersubjectivity is unwarranted. When a subject wants to trap an observer into wrongly imputing authenticity to a piece of manufactured evidence, his job will not be accomplished merely by putting his own sophistication as a standard for predicting how the observer will respond, Mead notwithstanding. . . . The game-theory assumption that one's opponent is exactly as smart as oneself is not a wise one in daily affairs. (1969:72–73)

Interactants have differential access to the informational resources of the group, and particular interactional moments are influenced by and, in turn, reaffirm the information differences among interactants.

Rosen (1984) provides a compatible perspective on the strategic interactional construction of social relationships with his Moroccan data. He suggests that Westerners "generally assume that when someone makes a statement about their relationship to another it is in some way connected to the truth— even if that connection is one of equivocation, dissimulation, or out-and-out lying" (1984:118). In contrast, Rosen's Moroccan informants do not judge statements as inherently true or false, valid or invalid. Rather, statements are deliberated and acted upon based on the moral, social, and economic obligations and on the relationship definitions they (potentially) establish. Statements are seen as assertive bids in the construction of interpersonal ties, not as factual utterances referring to some external set of reality conditions (cf. Austin, 1965, 1971; Searle, 1969). Thus, "If the utterance is accepted—if a relationship can be sucessfully shown to have flown from it—the statement can be judged as true, in that it has been adhered to, or false, in that it has been contravened" (Rosen, 1984:118–119). Chapter 4 of this book advances the notion that particular acts of communication serve to invoke larger contexts, frames, or codes, to which the acts contribute and from which the acts derive their significance. These larger contexts, frames, or codes implicate and entail subsequent courses of action for all participants, although the implications and entailments are subject to negotiation. Particular acts can thus be seen as bids in a continuous process that negotiates the applicability of contexts, frames, and codes and the terms of entailed behavior and relationship definitions.

Relationship Coherence. The from-above perspective on discourse concerns itself with constraints that are placed on utterance production apart from those related to either the structure or content of neighboring turns at talk. In part, the from-above perspective examines nontextual influences on, and features of, participants' verbalizations. In addition, the from-above perspective represents a departure from microinteractional studies of how actors produce talk, and emphasizes analyses of how actors construct continuous (and continuously meaningful) relationships through talk.

To return briefly to the brie and pet owner examples discussed above, it can be noted here that the speaker's behavior did affirm the existence of a quantity rule: "Do only what has to be done and no more." These examples illustrated something beyond this adherence as well: specifically, that social relationship construction can be seen to involve the sharing of (vicarious and direct) life experiences, the building up and organization of this relationship information, and the periodic utilization of such information during interaction. *There are certain classes of information that are, and perhaps must be, repeatedly invoked and deliberated upon by interactional partners.* These information repetitions—and the conversational codes that account for them—form part of what is described above as the conversational continuities of social relationships.

I have previously used the concept of *reportability requirements* to refer to these combined relationship and discourse patterns (Sigman, 1983a). Social relationships establish limitations on the objects of conversational attention by the comembers for both brief and extended discourse episodes, and reciprocally, social relationships are defined by and organized around particular discourse rules. Two types of reportability have been suggested.[3] First, there is information that must be proffered for conversational attention by any or all of the relationship members who have access to this information. Second, there is information that must be excluded from discourse. Berger and Luckmann refer to social stocks of knowledge that account for some of these conversational limitations in the following manner:

> An important element of my knowledge of everyday life is the knowledge of the relevance structures of others. Thus I "know better" than to tell my doctor about my investment problems, my lawyer about my ulcer pains, or my accountant about my quest for religious truth. (1967:45)

A similar set of distinctions is made by Rawlins (1983a) in his analysis of friendship. He writes that social relationships contain competing demands for disclosive and protective discourse:

> As more matters are enacted within a relationship, the aspects that remain private concerns for each person compose a pattern contrasting with the areas of open disclosure, observation, and commentary. (1983a:158)

These constraints provide for the differential and contextual relevance of speakers' discourse behavior (van Dijk, 1979). That is, they serve as macrostructures for relevance. They are also associated with the continuities of information exchanged in particular relationships, and with the ongoing rights and obligations individuals have toward each other.

A third constraint, *discourse askability,* can be proposed here. Certain information must be requested by relationship comembers during the course of their interactions with each other. If I am sick, for example, I expect my best friends, coworkers, and others with whom I have a "concerned" and "caring" relationship to ask me over the period of several days how I am doing. If I have lost my gold watch, I expect certain inquiries to be made concerning its whereabouts. If I am about to conclude a major business deal, I expect advice and questioning from colleagues and associates. Certainly, novel or special circumstances are not the only areas to be inquired about. Ongoing projects, activities, encounters, and the like may also figure into the contents of focused talk.

One of the discourse implications of askability is its status as a warrant for the introduction of acceptable topics into conversation at any moment.[4] That which must be considered when a conversation is begun is not simply background knowledge on a topic but also the degree to which discussion on that topic may be taken for granted and deemed appropriate. However, reportability and askability requirements are not merely social psychological or interactional constraints regarding individuals' contributions to conversation; they are also descriptions of the ongoing flow of messages constitutive of particular social relationships, situations, and organizations.[5]

Aragon similarly considers the existence of topic "routinization" in everyday discourse:

> It is a common phenomenon that a person will tell someone else something that he or she has already told that person at a previous time. The listener will often remind the speaker that these words have passed between them before and then the speaker will generally apologize and fault his or her memory. With respect to knowledge regarding the compartmentalization of discourse, this type of event may be reinterpreted. The forgetting of yesterday's utterances may have to do with decrepit memory but the reintroduction of topic, the critical issue, does not. Rather, given the present listener(s) and situation, the speaker may be permitted only a certain range of appropriate topics to discuss. If the range is not changing rapidly over time (which it rarely appears to do in most relationships) and if the classes of events which comprise that range have not been altered between the last and the present interactions of the participants, then the repetition of utterances becomes a not unlikely phenomenon. (1978:16)

Certain types of information flow (in the form of discourse topics) are continuous—sustained by the relationship requirements of offering the information and/or asking for it—and are thus appropriate for momentary reference or invocation (see also Pearce and Cronen, 1980).

Certain reportable (and askable) topics gain a special status as frequent objects of conversational attention by social actors. "Pet topics" may be as apparent for some interactants as nicknames are for others (Brown and Ford, 1961). Goffman (1959) observes that relationships develop favored story lines and team presentations.

Discourse behavior that adheres to reportability constraints thus functions as part of the mechanism for (1) partially defining the behavioral structure of a particular social relationship; (2) partially providing the information flow that comprises the relationship; and (3) partially sustaining the relationship. Rawlins writes, "Over the course of a relationship, friends acquire mutual knowledge of topics which reflect deep convictions or cause insecurity" (1983b:10). Also, "As a result, there is continuous dialectical interplay between the expressive and protective functions of communication in such enduring bonds" (1983b:12).

Thus, relational history and previous interactional experience do not merely constitute a background, a memory box, for discourse; rather, they can be seen to exist in the foreground of discourse behavior, as a treasure chest of information to be periodically opened, examined, and celebrated. Discourse participants have access to information sets and selectively invoke these to acknowledge and signal the continued existence and the current status of their social relationship. These moments of accessing the treasure chest and acknowledging some of its contents serve as a means for interactants to display the historic routes (and roots) of their relationship and its knowledge store (cf. Schutz and Luckmann's [1973] discussion of the "historization" of knowledge). Bormann's (1983) discussion of an aspect of organizational symbolization is appropriate here. He writes:

> Once the dynamic process of sharing a group fantasy creates symbolic convergence for a group of people, they will exhibit the *inside joke* syndrome. The inside joke is a communication incident in which a speaker alludes to a previously shared fantasy with a nonverbal signal or sign or verbal code word, slogan, label, name of hero or villain, or story summary. This brief and cryptic (to outsiders) message sparks a response appropriate in mood and tone to the original sharing response when the group members first created the consciousness associated with the fantasy. (1983:109; emphasis in original)

There are clear implications of either adhering to or deviating from such practices. For example, not to engage in expected behavior may serve to signal a disturbance, imbalance, or change in the relationship system (cf. Watzlawick, Beavin, and Jackson, 1967). In this regard, it is interesting that Kreckel writes, "There is a tendency for relatively stable information to be seen as context and for fast changing information to be conceived of as behaviour" (1981:20). However, as Bateson points out, "The essence and *raison d'être* of communication is the creation of redundancy, meaning, pattern, predictability, information, and/or the reduction of the random by 'restraint' " (1972:131–132).

Reportability requirements provide one possible framework of conversational expectations for the content of speakers' turns at talk. These conversational patterns produce a sort of relationship predictability concerning face-to-face conversation: certain topics are known to be safe and discussable; the reactions that different topics will engender can be anticipated; those topics which are capable of bridging difficult or uncomfortable interactional moments are so categorized and invoked at appropriate times; a set of interaction "fillers" is established and periodically used; and, against this background, participants invoke strategies for opening up or foreclosing on various other topics for discussion.

Zerubavel writes about the importance of those linguistic devices which symbolize relationship continuation thus:

> That people often terminate social encounters by making "bridging" references to the next ones (for example, "I'll see you later") is indicative of their need to convey to one another that the interactional void which is to follow should be regarded only as a temporary suspension of the relationship, and by no means as its end. (1979:39–40)

Similarly, Berger and Luckmann write that the social reality that individuals participate in is generally patterned so that it is experienced by them as uninterrupted:

> In order to maintain subjective reality effectively, the conversational apparatus must be continual and consistent. Disruptions of continuity or consistency *ipso facto* posit a threat to the subjective reality in question. . . . Various techniques to cope with the threat of discontinuity are . . . available. The use of correspondence to continue significant conversation despite physical separation may serve as an illustration. (1967:154)

In this light, the utilization of preferred and repeated topics during copresent interactional events, and of other discourse units that signal relationship equilibrium/disequilibrium, is another means for sustaining and referencing social interaction and social relationship continuities.

These observations further suggest that the primary or sole function of conversation is not necessarily new information transmission (cf. Malinowski, 1923; Simmel, 1949; Birdwhistell, 1970). Although reportability rules do specify conditions under which previously unfamiliar information must be conveyed by individuals with access to it, they also provide participants with a wealth of acceptable and repeatable topics, regardless of each topic's timeworn status.

It should be noted that I am not dealing here with the cognitive issue that certain background information may be taken for granted by speaker/hearers in the production and interpretation of verbal messages, although, of course, this function is acknowledged to be important. Rather, I am concerned in the present context with the articulation of a perspective for studying behavioral continuities, those repetitions across communication episodes of information that is, and/or is not, disseminated. These continuities enable talk to have a certain consistency and coherence through time, and are a foundation for maintaining social relationships.[6]

The Complexity of Reportability. There has been something of an analytic simplification up to this point regarding the structure of reportability rules. A full analysis of reportability constraints is beyond the more general scope of the present work, but two additional features can be briefly noted here.

First, the question of the relationship between what interactants' talk is about and what they are able to say it is about requires consideration. In a highly suggestive paper, Heritage and Watson (1979) comment that the topic(s) of a conversation may not be made explicit or become acknowledged by the participants until the conversation's terminal phase. They write that the overriding topic(s) are negotiated as the participants begin "formulating" the gist of their conversation. This negotiation involves formulation bids, and confirmatory or nonconfirmatory assessments, regarding the conversational topic, and is subject to continual elaboration. Heritage and Watson write:

> Members may, on occasion, formulate the sense or gist achieved thus far either in a conversation *in toto* or in some foregoing section of the conversation. Such formulations may, and frequently do, come to constitute clarifications, or demonstrations of comprehension or in-touchedness with the talk thus far. (1979:130)

From the standpoint of the present discussion, formulations can be seen to be based to some degree on prior and continuing topic constraints. In other words, they are demonstrations not simply of momentary comprehension, but of more general socially expected attention and understanding. Depending on the reportability and TFG delimitations of the participants' social relationship, particular formulations and/or formulations by particular interactants may hold sway over others.

The existence of formulation constraints can be clearly seen in the following extract from the People's Home ethnographic data (Sigman, 1985b, 1985/86, 1986):

(Noon, in living room area 4):
Edith Gould: I smell fish today.
Mrs. Bergman: No, I think it's grilled cheese. Some sort of cheese thing.
Gould: Oh, well, that's fine. It's better than that ——— they serve.
Bergman: Oh, yes. I don't like *that* at all.
Gould: And they put so much seasoning on it. That's the most fattening thing they can serve.
Bergman: I know.
Pearl Axelrod: I don't like it with all those spices.
Gould: Let's just say that we have nothing else to complain about, so we complain about the food.

Bergman: We're not complaining. We're just passing remarks.
Gould: That's true. Yes.
Axelrod: Yes.

Mrs. Gould, a recent entrant to People's Home at the time of this conversation, imputed the wrong label and evaluation to her peer group's sharing of seemingly negative comments about institutional food, and was quickly corrected on what the talk was "really all about." As I have suggested elsewhere, the nursing home residents generally adhered to a rule requiring them to project a positive and appreciative attitude toward life in the nursing home (see Sigman, 1985b). The acceptable formulation in the above conversation contributed to maintaining the spirit of this rule.

These observations suggest that the reportability requirements of social relationships are more patterned and complicated than previously envisioned. Specifically, there would appear to be information that is plus-or-minus reportable and plus-or-minus formulatable, a situation giving rise to the fourfold typology of information depicted in figure 2–1. Relationship-based constraints on conversational topics can thus be analyzed with regard to the reportability of the information featured in the discourse in conjunction with its formulatability.

A second consideration concerns the sharedness of conversationalists' information rules. The discussion on reportability in the previous section is based on an implicit (and simplistic) assumption of isomorphy or equivalence of the relationship participants' rules. While this heuristic simplification facilitates the initial description of reportability, it fails in the observation of conversational rules that are not fully shared by relationship comembers and of interactional

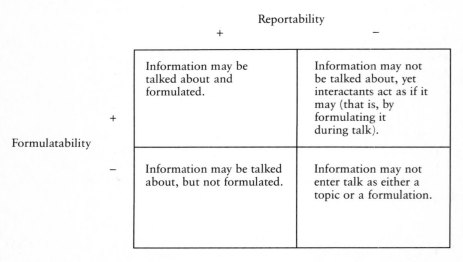

Figure 2–1. Information Configurations

events in which each person is bound by contrasting topic requirements. As a result of such behavioral asymmetries, the meaning of particular topic-related behavior for each relationship partner may not necessarily be identical. For example, Pearce and Cronen (1980) study the "convoluted interpersonal logic" of a couple in which the female partner, self-described as a "lazy person," requires a dominant comember to impel her to action, and the male partner, who considers himself "flexible" and "not dominant," takes as his goal the lessening of his partner's dependency. These contrasting logics lead to reports of different meanings for a recorded conversation concerned with the female partner's spiritless and unsuccessful job search:

> This episode culminates . . . where Dave gives explicit instructions for what Jan should do ["Well, you're getting up at eight o'clock and we're leaving the house at nine"]. Jan interprets this as an ultimatum that spurs her to action, and this is just what Jan wants. . . . For Dave, however, [this] act . . . counts as a backing down. "I'm telling her everything will be O.K., what's past doesn't matter, she can just start out fresh tomorrow." Thus Dave believes he is acting to move out of the dominating position by this act; he is no longer holding Jan's inactivity over her head. (Pearce and Cronen, 1980:276)

In order for the relationship described by Pearce and Cronen to endure, the partners apparently required or, at the very least, invoked ostensibly different meanings for the same utterance.[7] These competing meanings were associated with the different role definitions the partners assumed for themselves and/or assigned to the other.

These observations raise implications for research on reality construction processes of interpersonal relationships. Pearce and Cronen define social reality as "consist[ing] of the agreement among . . . persons about the characteristics of the we" (1980:285). Although they admit that there may be some nonisomorphy across participants' beliefs and that no one person possesses information regarding the total relational system, Pearce and Cronen nevertheless tend to conceive of social reality in terms of consensual group image. Recognizing that relationship members may be bound by contrasting reportability and formulatability constraints leads me to suggest that social reality consists of the *patterning* (not limited to isomorphism) of the beliefs and actions across participants of an interacting entity, for example, dyad, small group, or organization. Consistent with the general guidelines for social communication, this conceptualization is concerned not only with an individual's subjective experiencing of reality—his/her partial view of, and contribution to, social reality—but with the larger organization of beliefs and actions. Noteworthy in this conceptualization is the focus on (1) the various organizational schemes for members' beliefs, with isomorphy or agreement among partners representing only one such scheme, and (2) the various relationships between rule-governed conduct and rule-governed assessments or accounts of that conduct. Separate participants' accounts of relationship behavior neither validate nor invalidate each other; rather, they lend themselves to different structuring formats and are partials of these more inclusive patterns of social reality.

Summary

Interactional episodes can be studied in a manner that goes beyond a focus on the utterance-by-utterance linkages that speaker/hearers apparently make.[8] Continuities in the information exchanged by discourse and relationship participants can be observed over time and across interactional events. These continuities include the requirements that certain information be included in, and other information be excluded from, conversation. In addition, there is a preferred utilization of selected conversational topics. The from-above perspective on coherence is concerned with constraints on the contextual relevance, acceptability, and repetitiveness of utterances. Moreover, the from-above perspective suggests that such constraints are associated with distinguishable social configurations of information flow through time.

There is a "natural history" to verbal behavior; it can be studied through time and across individual episodes. Conversations can be seen as *enduring social enterprises,* and, therefore, are amenable to a from-above analysis.

Finally, it is suggested here that one of the functions of discourse behavior is to enable social actors to construct and rely upon behavioral predictabilities in integrating social relationships and in sustaining face-to-face interactional contact. The theme relating interaction and social relationships to a general theory of communication is continued in the next chapter.

Notes

1. The support for this research of the Green Island Foundation, administered by the Gerontology Center at the Pennsylvania State University, is gratefully acknowledged here.

2. Information may be individual, shared, or common, but not all unshared information is individual; see Kreckel (1981). We need studies of the information division of labor: in certain social systems, particular items of information may be "stored" in the occupants of particular statuses (Kaplan, 1981).

3. The term *reportability* is used so as to be consistent with Bateson's (1972) notion of messages exhibiting a "report," as well as a "command," function. Verbal reports are not about objective reality, however. I am in agreement with the treatment by Shotter (1985), who suggests that language does not report about the world but rather tells it, and, in the process of doing so, creates and constitutes it.

4. I am largely utilizing here an American conception of interpersonal relationships, one that stresses the importance of conversation. Ethnographic data suggest

that laconicity and taciturnity are defining features of relationships for other cultural groups. See Hymes (1974).

5. Pearce and Cronen (1980) refer to Keenan's (1973) data to discuss cross-cultural differences in the rules allowing or prohibiting "free" exchanges of information. They write:

> The reciprocal relation between communication and social institutions may be illustrated by the absurdity of transporting particular social institutions to other cultures. . . . The National Aeronautics and Space Agency (NASA) is a prototypically Western entity that simply could not function as it now does if staffed by members of the Malagasy culture, a people who have social rules prohibiting the free exchange of information (Keenan, 1973). (1980:87)

6. Traffic signals at roadway crossings need only make use of the most minimal of cues (a red and green light) to indicate the full range of actions expected of drivers at any given moment. More detailed messages, including signs proclaiming Wait for Green and Move Only on Green, are not necessary. Yet the study of any single elliptical message is not the same as that of the continuous flow of traffic-related signals and of the functions of particular repeated messages. The latter would be consistent with the goal of social communication research.

7. I write "ostensibly" here because David may have "known" in some fashion about the necessity of his being dominant in the relationship, although he did not explicitly acknowledge this. Repression can be seen in this light as a social communicational, rather than psychological, tool and process.

8. Starting research with micro units of behavior, as one does when approaching from-below, can be tedious because of the difficulties in ascertaining which multichannel behaviors properly "go together," that is, are related to each other and are part of a single hierarchical system, and in differentiating units from the same bodily part which are patterned not in relationship to each other but in relationship to units from other bodily parts. The continued development of kinesics has been hampered by the initial from-below starting point (cf. Birdwhistell, 1970).

3
Three Communication Orders

The discussion in the preceding chapters implies the existence of a close relationship between face-to-face interactional episodes and macrosocietal structures and processes. One of the hallmarks of social communication theory is the emphasis on interactional behavior as it serves to construct the participants' social relationships. The argument thus far points to a reflexive relationship between interactional behavior and social relationships, suggesting that each is to be defined by, and studied with reference to, the other. Nevertheless, the from-above perspective tends to confound the integrity of face-to-face interaction and social organization by intimating that one (the former) is partially constitutive of the other (the latter), that there is a strict hierarchical association between the two. This position fails to consider that relatively distinct units, for example, turn taking versus social ranking, serve as the respective minimal building blocks of interaction and social organization.

There has also been up to this point a lack of specificity in the various descriptions concerning the role of communication in the constitution of social reality and social structure, and concerning the precise relationship between communication and face-to-face interaction. The social communication focus on the informational aspects of social organization (see chapter 1) might be taken to mean that *communication* is but a processual or activity-oriented metaphor for *society*, the latter term having connotations of nondynamic structure. Such an interpretation harks back to Birdwhistell's (1970) earlier and rather vague description of how culture and communication are related to each other (also see Scheflen, 1968, 1974):

> From the point of view represented here, communication might be considered, in the broadest sense, as the active aspect of cultural structure. . . . Perhaps a more illuminating way of stating the case would be to say that I believe that the studies of those who look at patterned human interconnectedness, as it were, from above and derive *cultural generalizations* from their observations will produce data which will be coextant ultimately with data derived by those who study it from below and who derive *communicational generalizations*. (1970:251; emphasis in original)[1]

The implication that communication and society are, in a similar fashion, two sides of a single coin requires further consideration, especially as it leaves open the question of the relationship between face-to-face conduct and communication. Birdwhistell (1970) implies an ambiguous distinction between the two by writing that communication is the dynamic structure that enables interaction to transpire.

For these reasons, the present chapter assumes the task of systematically unpacking the relationship between and among interaction, communication, and social organization. The discussion is structured around the work of Erving Goffman (1959, 1961b, 1967, 1983a), the chief modern architect of an interactional approach to social life. More so than any other theorist whose work can be aligned with social communication theory (see Heilman, 1979), Goffman (1983a) is the most direct in establishing relevant terminological distinctions—in this case, through his separation of the "interaction order" from the remainder of social life. The discussion in this chapter proceeds in this manner: first, Goffman's distinctions are described, and second, certain inadequacies of the terms are presented; finally, amendations to Goffman's scheme are proposed which provide a more detailed articulation of interaction, communication, and social organization, and which are applicable to some of the cross-cultural data on multifunctional behavior currently available.

Goffman's Interaction Order

Goffman's 1982 presidential address to the American Sociological Association represents the culmination and, in many respects, the most explicit presentation of his concern for the micromomentary details of everyday interactional life. The essay represents a clear and even bold attempt—Goffman (1983a) admits, for example, that not everyone shares his obsession for an interactionally focused sociology—to provide a theoretical foundation for separating the study of interaction from social structural investigations. Specifically, it is an attempt in the spirit of Durkheim (1938) to treat interaction as an order, an integral entity or domain whose constitutive processes and elements are capable of being distinguished from other orders, and whose delineation enables and justifies comparative analyses of societal groupings and historical periods. Goffman does not claim that the abstraction of interaction is more real than the abstraction of society (or social structures), only that the same principles for abstracting conceptual entities and treating them sui generis can be applied to both. Interpreting Goffman's general argument as developed in earlier works, Heilman writes, "The social occasion is dialectic in character in that it both depends upon and overpowers the interactants. In their coming together they have inevitably brought upon themselves the third partner of society" (1979:229). This third partner exists as a "world available whenever the individual decides to dip into it" (Goffman, 1961b:41).[2] Moreover, this third partner exists apart from the particular moment or interactants: "We cannot say the worlds [of face-to-face interaction] are created on the spot, because . . . use is usually made of traditional equipment having a social history of its own in the wider society and a wide consensus of understanding regarding the meanings that are to be generated from it" (Goffman, 1961b:27–28).

Returning to his oft expressed concern for the sensory availability of persons in a geographically and temporally bounded location, Goffman's presidential address defines interaction as "that which uniquely transpires in social situations, that is, environments in which two or more individuals are physically in one another's response presence" (1983a:2). Earlier, he writes, "[Face-to-face] interaction may be roughly defined as the reciprocal influence of individuals upon one another's action when in one another's immediate physical presence" (Goffman, 1959:14). The following are some of the defining features of the order that Goffman suggests gives rise to face-to-face interaction:

1. As noted, interactional events are circumscribed in space and time.

2. These events require the behavioral and cognitive involvement of the several participants toward each other.

3. As a consequence of the requirements for involvement and attention, interactional events are vulnerable to the passing of time and to the exigencies of moment-by-moment happenings—for example, postponements and interruptions can serve to alter the development and progression of interaction.

4. Being in the physical, and thus interactional, presence of others provides interactions with a "promissory, evidential character" (Goffman, 1983a:3)—the participants' appearance and manner exhibit information about their identities, statuses, relationships, intentions, goals, degrees of involvement in the unfolding event(s), and so on, although such information may be subject to manipulation and falsification.

5. Interactional copresence requires devices for the coordination of all persons' activities, whether the task(s) at hand are defined collaboratively and jointly or separately and only adjacently.

The interaction order is viewed neither as the surface behavioral manifestation of macrosocietal processes nor as a subordinate level in a hierarchy culminating in macrosocietal structures. Goffman (1983a) acknowledges that the interaction order may have an effect on social organization and, conversely, that particular patterns of social organization may on occasion "press" against the interaction order. Nevertheless, for Goffman, awareness of such influences does not warrant softening the claim that interaction represents a distinct and distinguishable order. The interaction order and the social structure are presumed to comprise units and organizing principles that are unique and specific to each; it is the separate features of interaction and social structure which are the legitimate target of sociological research, rather than the relatively minor points of intersection or mutual influence. For example, Goffman notes that "insofar as a complex organization comes to be dependent on particular personnel. . . , then the daily sequence of social [interactional] situations on and off the job . . . in which these personages can be injured or abducted are also situations in which their organizations can suffer" (1983a:8). In other words, there is a potential here for interactional contingencies to give rise to social structural and social organizational contingencies. However, the potentials for such "risk" are "of no great conceptual interest" (Goffman, 1983a:8).

More compelling in the assessment of an intimate connection between interaction and social structure, and possibly more damaging to Goffman's separatist argument, "is the obvious fact that a great deal of the work of organizations . . . is done face-to-face, [and] requires being done in this way" (1983a:8). Decision-making encounters, the coordination and aggregation of physical labor contributed by different individuals, and institutional gatekeeping episodes (see chapter 4; also Erickson and Shultz, 1982) are clear cases in which what occurs through interaction reverberates social structurally. Nevertheless, Goffman rejects the implications of these observations, and, in the process, argues against the symbolic interactionist school (Blumer, 1969), whose tenets he has often been associated with by others (see Collins, 1985). Specifically, Goffman writes, "This has led some to argue reductively that all macrosociological features of society, along with society itself, are an intermittently existing composite of what can be traced back to the reality of encounters—a question of aggregating and extrapolating interactional effects" (1983a:8). Goffman's carefully phrased yet unequivocal criticism of this stance is important and warrants lengthy citation:

> I find these claims uncongenial. For one, they confuse the interactional format in which words and gestural indications occur with the import of these words and gestures, in a word, they confuse the situational with the merely situated. When your broker informs you that he has to sell you out or when your employer or your spouse informs you that your services are no longer required, the bad news can be delivered through a sequestered talk that gently and delicately humanizes the occasion. Such considerateness belongs to the resources of the interaction order. At the time of their use you may be very grateful for them. But the next morning what does it matter if you had gotten the word from a wire margin call, a computer readout, a blue slip at the time clock, or a terse note left on the bureau? How delicately or indelicately one is treated during the moment in which bad news is delivered does not speak to the structural significance of the news itself. (Goffman, 1983a:8–9)

Goffman's analysis of this situation is subtle: he is suggesting here that interactional effects are situational, while social effects are transcendent, not easily reduced to a particular context, location, activity, or situation. Moreover, Goffman is arguing that there is no clear mapping, no one-to-one relationship, between interactional and social effects, between the distinctions and processes of relevance to each domain. Much of what occurs interactionally does not have social structural import.[3] Much of what is definitional and constitutive of the interaction order does not find its way into the arrangement of the relevant units and procedures of the social structure.

The connection of events, practices, and behavior units across the interaction order and social structure is best described, according to Goffman (1983a), using the terms *nonexclusive linkage* and *loose coupling*. Either domain can be observed making distinctions that do not form part of the technical vocabulary of the other; the two domains may provide elaborations or distinctions for a similar substantive arena, for example, power, yet the differentiations across domains need not be identical or intersect with each other. The following citation attempts to illustrate how social structural distinctions—in this case, gender and organizational status—can be made relevant to the interaction order, although these distinctions do not initially "belong" to the latter:

> From the perspective of how women in our society fare in informal cross-sexed talk, it is of very small moment that (statistically speaking) a handful of males, such as junior executives, have to similarly wait and hang on other's [sic] words—albeit in each case not many others. From the point of view of the interaction order, however, the issue is critical. For one, it allows us to try to formulate a role category that women and junior executives (and anyone else in these interactional circumstances) share, and this will be a role that belongs *analytically* to the interaction order, which the categories women and junior executives do not. (Goffman, 1983a:11–12; emphasis in original)

This collapsing of categories as the analyst moves from consideration of situated interaction to nonsituated features of social structure gives rise to the following methodological principle:

> It is easy enough, then, and even useful, to specify in social structural terms who performs a given act of deference or presumption to whom. In the study of the interaction order, however, after saying that, one must search out who else does it to whom else, then *categorize the doers with a term that covers them all,* and similarly with the done to. And one must provide a technically detailed description of the forms involved. (Goffman, 1983a:12; emphasis added)

Goffman thus exploits his earlier notion of "transformation" (Goffman, 1961b, 1974) in order to sketch the affinities and linking processes between interaction and social structure. The analytic apparatus for relating the various distinctions exists in the form of "a set of transformation rules, or a membrane selecting how various externally relevant social distinctions will be managed within the interaction" (1983a:11). Goffman sees transformation rules "in the geometrical sense of that term, these being rules, both inhibitory [establishing what participants must not attend to] and facilitating [what they must recognize], that tell us what modification in shape will occur when an external pattern of properties is given expression inside the encounter" (1961b:33). The inside-outside, boundary metaphor operating here is important to note; it points to a particular way of conceptualizing and studying interactional events, specifically, by requiring that the spatial and temporal limits coincident with the interactants' physical copresence also serve as the analytic limits for the interactional event itself (see Sigman, 1983a). So, for example, a person's *social status* as a Jew, black, handicapped veteran, female, and so on will need to be transformed into a *participation status* (Goffman, 1974)—such as interactional nonperson—if this status is to enter into, and be behaviorally relevant to, the unfolding sequence.

Goffman's brief sketch of the transformational process would seem to require the following abilities and activities on the part of interactants: (1) the perception of externally relevant social distinctions, that is, categories that are derived from outside the interactional event; (2) the recognition of internally relevant transforms, that is, interactional equivalents; and (3) the application of some translation machinery to convert the first set of distinctions into the second set in order to establish behavioral guidelines consistent with the latter.

In an early work, Goffman (1961b) suggests that what becomes relevant for participants' attention within the boundaries of the interaction may be highly circumscribed and delimited. Encounters are sustained by rules of relevance and irrelevance for a variety of socially defined attributes—attributes that are otherwise meaningful outside the encounter. One of Goffman's examples is drawn from the world of games and can be used to show that definitions of persons' status are not the only features that contrast what transpires within interaction with what is relevant to other domains of social life. Goffman (1961b) observes that only certain attributes of the game pieces for, say, chess (for example, king versus pawn), and not others (wood versus gold), are relevant to the structuring and carrying out of the game. While the wood-versus-gold distinction may be salient and applicable to some other social "game" (for example, status conferral on persons), and may momentarily be used to shift the focus of attention away from the interactional episode during the course of a game, it is not a fundamental constituent of the chess game. In other words, there are certain abstract features that define and constitute the game qua structured interaction, and there are others that are peripheral to it (albeit central to the doing of some other domains of social life).

It is important to note that Goffman is not alone in his attempt to build a sui generis argument for interaction structure. Scheflen (1965a), for one, provides a comparable view when writing that the programs or sequential structures that guide the therapeutic encounters he studied can be separated from the participants' social identities. Scheflen suggests, for example, that in examining the rule-governed organization of therapeutic episodes, that is, focusing on the interaction order, the social actors who perform particular behaviors are interchangeable and their social identities do not intrude on the organization:

> Communicative units are rarely performed by one person when others are also present who know the routine. . . . In fact, when in a pattern a given behavior is called for at a certain point it may not matter who performs it. If it is performed the sequence continues; if it is not the pattern repeats, halts or takes another direction.
>
> At one level it did not matter whether Whitaker or Malone [the therapists] made the bowl [gesture] or who spoke during its performance. (Scheflen, 1965a:31)

Scheflen hedges by saying that this separation is possible only when focusing on certain analytic levels:

> It may make a difference who performs a given unit when that person has a special status. For instance, a monitor may not correct a deviancy unless it is performed by a high status figure. (1965a:31; original italics omitted here)

Of course, one of the problems here is exactly what is meant by a "level." I will return to a consideration of the relationship between levels and orders in the last two sections of the chapter.

Anticipating the discussion below, the following critical observations can be noted here. While it may be true that interactional events are guided by a structure, or belong to an order, that is distinct from other structuring or ordering domains, it can be argued that "real-time," observable communication behavior contains units that are multifunctional and constrained by more than one set of rules or principles. While chess is not defined by the material pieces, a chess game is not usually played without such material pieces. While the bowl gesture is not delineated with regard to who performs it, its production nevertheless requires someone to accomplish this. The various material pieces of particular chess games and the diverse persons employing a bowl gesture on specific occasions have contrastive meaning for interaction which can be explored—or, at the very least, the conceptual possibility that there is contrastive meaning to be studied must remain open. The following sections elaborate this commentary on Goffman's approach to face-to-face interaction, and then propose modifications that seem more sensitive to the multifunctional nature of communication behavior.

Commentary on the Interaction Order

That there is no simple, one-to-one correspondence between distinctions concerned with interaction and social organization does not seem to be a sufficient criterion for precluding the systematic study of the two domains of social life in relation to each other, or relegating the scholarly task solely to the discovery of transformation rules. Both these solutions essentially leave the interaction order intact and analytically isolated from the rest of social life.[4] That such correlation is neither simple nor unitary owes much to the creative insights of social scientists who are able to posit behavioral multifunctionality and analyze multiple layers of "work" that apparently need to be accomplished during moments of face-to-face interaction (see below). Indeed, given the delineation of social communication research topics expressed in chapter 2, the relationship between units of interaction and of social structure is at the forefront of investigatory attention. However, as seen above, this enterprise is given little analytic weight within a framework that unambiguously defines interaction as a unique and integral order unto itself. Communication provides for multiple meanings and meaning structures beyond the interactional; it is unclear how these should be addressed in a theory that so deeply cuts a separation between the interactional and social structural realms of everyday life.

One way to address these concerns is to question the ontological status of social relationships and of other features of social organization, for example, power, rank, the division of labor. Goffman (1983a), it can be recalled, suggests that social structures cannot be reduced to the patterns of behavior that are manifest in, and constitutive of, face-to-face interactional engagements. The processes of what can be considered to be the "social order"—that is, the order constituting social structure—transcend the situationally bound and located features of the interaction order, although both are comprised of supraindividual units, structures, and dynamics.[5] An interactant's performance of an interaction order unit, say, a turn-requesting signal (see Sacks, Schegloff, and Jefferson, 1974; Duncan, 1972; Sigman, 1981), must be understood within the context of the total repertoire of behaviors that serve to organize interaction both sequentially and hierarchically. A turn-requesting signal exists as the same degree and kind of abstraction as an indirect speech act (Ervin-Tripp, 1976; Searle, 1969), a topic-transition device (Keenan and Schieffelin, 1976), a face formation (Kendon, 1977), and the like. According to Goffman (1983a), these various units and procedures exist in a realm removed from that concerned with the construction of power differential between/among participants, gender identification, social relationship obligations, and so on. Yet there is a problem here in that this second group of features and processes, which can be said to constitute the social order, exist only as patterns of observable behavior, albeit not situationally bound or structured in the same way that the turn-taking activities may be. Social order units depend on architectural, artifactual, gestural, olfactic, vocalic, and other distinctions—distinctions that are meaningful—as do interaction order units; both are created, sustained, and enacted through multichannel semiotic (behavioral) codes. As Giddens correctly observes, "So-called 'microsociological' study does not deal with a reality that is somehow more substantial than that with which 'macrosociological' analysis is concerned" (1984:xxvi).

While it may be true that only some of the behavior units characteristic of the social order facilitate and are relevant to the construction of face-to-face interactional events, nevertheless some (unspecified) portion of the behavior of the social order appears and takes on relevance during moments involving the physical and sensorial availabilities of persons. Goffman may be correct in suggesting that the dynamics of the social order cannot be explained by reductive appeal to the constituent features and procedures of the interaction order, and that comprehension of the grammar of interaction requires the examination of interaction-specific units. Nevertheless, neither the interaction nor the social order exists apart from observable behavior.

This critical perspective does not imply that the behavior units of interaction and of social organization are isomorphic or that their structuring principles and formats are identical. More important, however, such a perspective does not inevitably and categorically commit us to reject the possibility of shared units for the two orders. As elaborated upon below, the present conception leaves open the possibility that some units and processes may be unique to each order, while simultaneously suggesting that there may be partially overlapping units and processes as well. This presupposes that the analyst is constrained to proceed only on the basis of his/her observations of behavior.

Goffman (1983a) suggests that the behaviors that mark power differentials, to take just one feature of what is here considered the social order, are not those which structure the focused interactional moment. What the analyst can see to be symptomatic of a power differential between persons, for example, between a black and a white participant, does not necessarily contribute units that organize and order the event under study *as an interactional event.* This seems only partially accurate. The interaction order can be envisioned as providing numerous options or alternatives for engaging in face-to-face interaction, for example, ratifying participants, taking turns, sequencing utterances, and so on. The particular option or options produced and invoked by the participants at each moment are constrained by multiple factors. Social structural considerations, as well as those resulting from momentary interactional exigencies—for example, which sensory modality is most readily usable in the particular environment—delimit the actual range of options that is appropriate at that time, and may also determine the particular option that is invoked.

Goffman acknowledges the constraint that the social order places on momentary selections of interaction order units, but he does not pursue the implications of this observation or give it extensive place in his scheme: "Social structures don't 'determine' culturally standard displays, merely help select from the available repertoire of them" (1983a:11). He suggests that precedence and priority in seating, queuing, accessing interacting groupings, interrupting coparticipants, and so on "are interactional in substance and criteria" (1983a:11).

While this may certainly be true, it seemingly fails to recognize the importance of what is transpiring coincidentally for the social structural and interaction orders.

Consider a hypothetical situation in which participant A considers participant B to be "social dirt" but also considers him/herself to be under an interactionally based obligation—say, by dint of the sharing of a railway compartment—to generate, albeit briefly, some conversational topic. The two considerations, one derived from the social order, the other from the interaction order, jointly constrain the initiation, duration, termination, and substance of the focused talk. If each order were studied independently, it might be possible to see a number of options for behaving that do not materialize when the two orders are studied jointly; however, real-time interactional events are not so singularly controlled. For example, one means of signaling one's disdain toward, and rejection of, some copresent other might involve a refusal to ratify the other by entering into interaction focused on some topic. However, if at a given point in time, the interactional obligation to generate a topic is given precedence by the social superior, then the avoidance mechanism is effectively eliminated from the applicable behavioral repertoire. In other words, the actual and perceived obligation to generate a topic constrains one procedure otherwise employable for conveying one's impressions of another as social inferior, for example, through nonratification. A behavior belonging to the respective subrepertoires of both orders will most likely be sought for production. The obligation to keep persons in their social places while engaging them in ratified talk yields a short list of potential topics for discussion—excluding such ones as would build greater similarity or intimacy between the speakers. In brief, the existence of an interactional slot to be filled—in this case, the specification that there be focused interaction, and, therefore, some access ritual/topic generation— overlaps to some extent with a slot within the social order for presenting and sustaining status differences.

It should be pointed out that I am not claiming to be developing here a model of the cognitive steps involved in the selection and generation of behavior units. Rather, this discussion is intended to suggest some of the logical considerations—that is, the logical relations between the two orders—that must be embedded in such a model. The model must account for the substantive constraints and contributions provided by both interaction and social order rules. An alternative description to the one above—in which the performance selection was made from a short list derived from the shared resources of the two repertoires—might be to suggest that the participant's knowledge of the interaction order provides an initial set of possibilities, which are then evaluated by some mechanism consistent with meanings contained by, and to be transmitted as part of, the social order. Other decision models are possible as well.

Various studies exemplify the importance of considering multiple constraints on behavior and multiple connections between behavior and the two orders. Rosen's (1984) ethnographic fieldwork in Morocco indicates that social relationships between persons are not necessarily fixed a priori; they are open to considerable negotiation and strategic construction during the course of a face-to-face engagement. He writes:

> Using a vast array of resources—his inherent ties of kinship, his control over physical and symbolic reserves, his capacity to cajole or manipulate others, his rhetorical skills and force of personality—he [the Moroccan] forges a range of personal, contractual, and often ad hoc ties to others that are as distinctive in their particular patterning as they are typical in their modes of construction. (1984:112)

The search for information about the other, an attempt to typify one's coparticipant (cf. Schutz and Luckmann, 1974), thus becomes a critical feature of all interaction. The initial elements of the greeting, for example, are employed by participants to situate each other socially so as to know how to conduct themselves next, and, more important, to assess the relationship obligations that could and might be developed.

An even clearer example of how interaction structures are used, and are usable, to facilitate the forging of social relationships and indebtedness is provided by Irvine (1974) in her ethnographic description of Wolof greetings. The Wolof require a greeting and brief period of focused interaction to occur among all persons who are acquainted and who find themselves in each other's sensory presence, for example, at the market or crossing a field. The greeting is structured so as to be produced dyadically, and consists of a sequence of stereotyped questions, responses, and laudatory exclamations to Allah. Unlike the American greeting, which allows for reciprocal exchanges of "hello," stereotyped enquiries and pleasantaries, and so on, the Wolof greeting clearly and unilaterally assigns the dyadic speakers to either the initiator-questioner or respondent role. Who takes the "lower hand," as it were, to initiate the greeting and follow through with the routinized questions, has clear implications for how the interactants' respective social statuses are being defined:

> A set of associations emerges concerning the two parties to a greeting, associations which recall cultural stereotypes of noble and griot (or noble and low-caste) behavior:

> | Initiator | : | Speaker | : | Moving | : | Low status | : | Griot. |
> |---|---|---|---|---|---|---|---|---|
> | Respondent | | Nonspeaker | | Stationary | | High status | | Noble |

> The Wolof notion that the low-ranking person travels about more and talks more than the high-status person is here replicated in the status-differentiated roles of the greeting. (Irvine, 1974:173)

Although there are ways to strategically "self-lower" or "self-elevate" while greeting, the performance of the greeting structure functions in general both to initiate focused interaction and to define the relative ranking of the participants.

A third example concerning behavioral multifunctionality can be briefly noted here. In research I have conducted on the turn exchange system, a modification of the one-speaker-at-a-time rule was proposed (Sigman, 1980b, 1981). Videotape analysis indicated that interactants make use of subtle cues that function to initiate and sustain conversational fission, the state in which a single conversation dissolves into multiple subsidiary conversations and several speakers simultaneously address several auditors (see the discussion of "schism" by Sacks, Schegloff, and Jefferson [1974] and of "fragmentation" by Parker [1984]). While fission functions to organize the flow of talk and thus belongs to the interaction order, it is also used by participants—whether consciously or not is not at present the issue—to control each other's knowledge states and/or relative status within a group or institution (see Sigman, 1980b; Sigman and Wendell, 1986). Fission thus constitutes a feature of the social order as well.

In brief, then, it appears that there is a close relationship between interaction and social order units. How should such observations be handled by the communication analyst? What are the implications of Goffman's transformational approach which make it unacceptable in light of the above discussion? Why not adopt it?

First, it is my belief that should the notion of transformation rules be fully developed, it would prove to be exceedingly complex, and, moreover, inconsistent with other processes that Goffman (1983a) isolates as being part of interactional encounters. In addition, it fails to consider that at least for some enthnographic data (for example, Irvine, 1974), interaction order considerations and meanings are directly tied to social order ones, and vice versa.

It is suggested above that the notion of transformational procedures from the social order to the interaction order involves a three-step process of perception, recognition, and translation. This first approximation of a transformational model, while consistent with Goffman's own sketch, is nevertheless inadequate. In order for interactants to perceive the existence and potential applicability of social order distinctions, it would seem that they must first rely on behavioral cues that are directly apparent (sensible) within the encounter, that is, are part of the evidential character of the interaction. These behavioral cues will be glossed—whether subsequently or simultaneously is an empirical question—by labels that form part of the categorial repertoire of the social order. In other words, behavioral cues that exist and are displayed *within* the confines of the particular interaction must come to be interpreted and placed as part of a system of meanings that are *outside* the confines of the particular interaction. Some transformation or interpretive rule is needed to accomplish this. However, in order for the transformational process specifically delineated by Goffman to be initiated, there must also be an awareness on the part of the interactants of some relationship between these external categorizations and potential interactional equivalents. The transformational mechanism then filters or translates the social order categorizations, producing interaction order ones.

Thus, the full scope of a transformational treatment would seem to require social actors to begin (both behaviorally and cognitively) within the boundaries of the interactional event (evidential facet of the interaction order), to move outside these boundaries (the social order), and to return to a vocabulary for action which is acceptable and approprite within these boundaries (the interaction order).

In addition to the rather cumbersome nature of the analytic apparatus outlined here, a transformational treatment appears flawed in that it must rely on both the interaction and social orders for application, that is, on dual sets of transformations, and therefore confounds the supposed boundary between the two orders.

Moreover, it would be difficult to include such an approach in the present statement of social communication theory, because it does not appear to be fully consistent with, or to make use of, the notions of partials, partial contributions, and multifunctionality introduced in chapter 1 and employed above in the discussion of turn-taking and greeting behavior.

Rather than social order discriminations being transformed into interaction order ones, so that the semantics of the former are translated into that of the latter, I suggest that choices in the one realm are directly related to and controlled by the dynamics of this first realm, and that choices in the second realm are directly related to and controlled by the dynamics of this second realm. Unless a transformational treatment were able to retain some residue of meaning from the original social order categorization subsequent to the application of the transformation rules, the unit(s) produced during interaction would be semantically stripped and limited. That is to suggest, the social order meanings would be vitiated once the transformational process had been set in motion.

There are separable constraints that each order places on behavioral production; a particular interactional event comprises units that are constrained to varying degrees by each order and that are meaningful in light of each order. There are at least two ways to conceive of this. In some cases, it can be observed that the dynamics of the interaction and social orders converge, producing some combined constraint on the appearance of whatever behavior unit does appear in the real-time situation. Alternatively, and as suggested above, the interaction and social orders can provide separate limitations on the range of behavioral options, with the unit ultimately produced being drawn only from a short list comprising the options shared by or overlapping the two repertoires. In either case, it is potentially misleading to assume that one constraint has been transformed into another, since the behavior that is actually performed "has" meaning derived from its place in *both* orders. The earlier discussion of how fission is used both to control topic progression and to indicate each person's status vis-à-vis the others and the information being shared is a good illustration of this point. Engaging in fission-related behavior is significant for what it accomplishes both interactionally and socially.

Such multiple constraints are to be found not only for interaction and social relationship construction. An interdependence between the interaction order and what might be considered the economic order (or, more accurately, economic processes of the social order) can also be studied. Economic processes are concerned with the allocation of resources—especially goods and services—throughout the social system. For example, the economics of the clinician's daily round limit the temporal duration of therapist-patient interaction such that, at fifty minutes into the psychoanalytic session, the proferring of termination behaviors for the session is required. Interestingly, it is clearly the economic processes that influence and define a crucial feature of the interaction order with this example. The termination behavior may belong to some extent to the repertoire for behavior outlined by, and constituting, the interaction order; yet the placement of the termination behavior in relation to the overall temporal scheduling and ecological demarcation of therapist-patient copresence is a structural feature of the medical world's social-economic order.[6] The performance of the termination behavior when it does in fact occur, at fifty minutes into the session, properly belongs to *both* the interaction and social-economic orders (as well as one other—see below); conversely, the interaction and social-economic orders are both constituted by the behavior in the fifty-minute session and at the precise moment concluding the fifty-minute session.

It is Goffman's (1983a) decision to restrict his examinations to the *local significance of behavioral forms* which is ultimately at issue here. The function of a unit must be found, according to Goffman, within the boundaries of the space-time copresence, not extra-situationally. Yet many of the behaviors occurring during face-to-face interactional engagements do not appear to be consequential wholly within the space-time boundaries of the event. As a result, interactionally bound analyses do not exhuast such behavior's functions. Moreover, some of the behaviors transpiring within an interactional event are not constitutive of that event, but rather contribute functions primarily to the social structure. Yet the likely appearance and potential for social structural interpretation is facilitated by face-to-face contact. The dandy's silk handkerchief is social structurally—as well as economically—significant when it lies inside its owner's dresser drawer; but it "broadcasts" to a wider audience on the occasion of copresent interaction by its owner with others. The process by which the interaction order facilitates and engenders opportunities for social structural effects to be worked out, that is, for social order devices to be placed into the interaction, requires examination. This example further implies that what is labeled interaction during the real-time event may be constituted by behaviors that are patterned singularly by one abstract order or the other. In other words, *interaction*—a real-time phenomenon—must be separated from the *interaction order*—an abstracted category of behaviors. There is no a priori reason to assume that behavior units occurring in the same delimited, focused interaction necessarily contribute to, and are governed by, the same behavioral order, level, or hierarchy. As noted in chapter 2, one problem with microanalytic, from-below research is that it provides no basis for knowing whether temporally and/or spatially adjacent behavioral forms belong to the same coding system (be this an order, level, or hierarchy) or contribute in nonoverlapping fashion to separate ones. From-above research, in contrast, enables the researcher to establish tentative streams of behavior and to list out the kinds of behavior units likely to form part of each stream without regard to channel derivation.

A final critical observation on Goffman's work concerns social structural constraints on the appearance of opportunities for participants' engagement in particular copresent interactional moments and/or performance of selected behavioral forms. This is different from the criticism above, which concerns the regulation by the social order of the choice between alternative units otherwise governed by the interaction order. Rather, I am concerned here with how the social order shapes opportunities for the instantiation of the interaction order. Given a person's position in the social structure, there may be differential access to repertoires of interactional behaviors and events. In other words, behavioral repertoires for interaction can be seen to be delimited by, and, in turn, to be reinforced by, one's place in the society or group. The implication of this is that the instantiation of the interaction order may be dependent upon access rules—for categories of behaviors, persons, and events—defined by the social order. This relationship between interaction and social orders is not well accounted for by a transformational treatment, since it is not simply the case that social order features need some translation in order to appear interactionally. In contrast, I am suggesting here that on occasion, the instigation or initiation of interaction may be dependent upon social order availabilities of persons and contacts between and among persons. Instead of a transformation rule, a "generative" rule is called for, a mechanism specifying conditions—in this case, ones derived from the social order—for the generation of a particular behavioral phenomenon—in this case, an interactionally based encounter. Once again, it can be assumed that the appearance of the various units is consequential within the interaction and across the social structure.

In concluding this section, it may be useful to situate the above observations on the nature of the interaction order in relation to MacCannell's (1983) more general criticism of Goffman's sociology (see also Gouldner, 1970; Giddens, 1984). MacCannell writes:

> This is the crisis-point in Goffman's social theory—for his embrace of the phenomenological sign that is restricted to *immediate presence* and the self-representation of the signifier coincides with what is most distinctive, in the sense of odd, and least defensible in Goffman's work: namely, his insistence that face-to-face interaction can be marked off as a separate field of study. . . . When viewed from any vantage point except that of the phenomenological sign [the sign as it is dependent on immediate appearance, perception, and presence], this is a preposterous project. If there was ever a subject matter

enmeshed in and determined by institutional arrangements, class structure, ethnic and community traditions, psychological quirks, etc., etc., it is face-to-face interaction. An opposite case for the absolutely contingent quality of interaction would have been easier to make. Only Goffman's genius for detail and sheer energy of production made face-to-face interaction seem complete in itself, and then only for the duration of his writing about it. (MacCannell, 1983:25; emphasis in original)

It is suggested above that while the interaction order can be considered a domain unto itself, its units are dependent on other domains for their appearance, and some mechanism must be posited to account for the multiple meanings and functions that interactional forms contribute to the interactional moment and to the social grouping. While there is a sense in which certain features of face-to-face interaction have a sui generis quality to them, there is nevertheless a concern to include this observation within a broader approach to communication which emphasizes multifunctionality.

Relations and Three Orders

Slots, Partials, and Orders

A distinction can be drawn between the interaction order as an abstract system of rules governing units and procedures that create face-to-face interaction, and real-time instantiations, invocations, or productions of this order. During actual interactional performances, the behavior that realizes the abstract order may also serve as partials associated with other orders. While the interaction order in the abstract may contain units and unit relationships that uniquely belong to this one order, the actual flow of interactional behavior at any one moment exhibits units and unit relationships that differentially, yet multiply, contribute to several orders. This distinction between the interaction order and interaction, or, more generally, between a behavioral order and behavior, echoes the distinction in chapter 1 between communication as *structure* versus as *activity,* and adumbrates one in chapter 4 between communication as *code* versus as *(invoking) process.* The former term in each pair refers to the total set of rules regulating and facilitating behavioral production, while the latter represents the continuous moments of behavioral production that selectively make use of or invoke the code. Cronen, Pearce and Tomm similarly reflect on the dual nature of communication behavior:

> Structure refers to organizations of meaning and repertoires of acts that persons possess. Action refers to conjointly produced sequences of behaviors. The relationship between structure and action is reflexive. Structure emerges from patterns of coordinated action and turns back upon those patterns guiding them. (1985:205)

(For a different definition of *structure* and *pattern,* see chapter 5.)

It is when the interaction order is actually lived, that is, when interaction is produced, that it becomes difficult for the analyst (and participants) to distinguish units that are unique to this one order and not multiply enmeshed in other behavioral orders. During the course of an actor's behaving in a face-to-face episode, social structural distinctions are not simply transformed into interactionally relevant ones in order to be performed. Rather, at each performance moment, behavior is seen to be accounted for, and generated by, both the interaction and social orders—a third order, the semiotic, is proposed below. These considerations lead to a non–apriori conceptualization of the relationship between the interaction and social orders; they allow different degrees and types of coupling (in the general sense of mutual constraint) to be empirically determined for particular communities, categories of persons, and interactional events.

Selecting this approach, it then becomes a legitimate research issue within social communication for researchers to specify precise linkages of interaction and social structure both synchronically and diachronically. Certain groups specify a comparatively rigid coupling between interaction and social structure. The degree of rigidity can be assessed via Hall's (1984) notion of high- and low-context cultures. According to Hall, "High context or low context refers to the amount of information that is in a given communication as a function of the context in which it occurs" (1984:229). Communication in the high-context culture tends to rely on background, taken-for-granted knowledge; message structure is largely "restricted" (Bernstein, 1975). In contrast, low-context cultures pattern more explicit or "elaborated" (Bernstein, 1975) messages, relying minimally on background context(s) for interpretation. Hall suggests an association between high/low context message structuring and interpersonal acquaintanceship: "People who know each other over a long period of years will tend to use high context communication" (1984:229). In other words, in the low-context mode, in which background and taken-for-granted knowledge is less available, the social order is likely to make more extensive and explicit use of behavior performed during interaction. Cross-cultural data reveal a variety of patterns in this regard.

There are a number of ways in which the relationship between high/low contextuality and interpersonal relationship can be observed. For example, the social order can be seen to serve as a primary constraint on the interaction order. Groups that embed status markers and like honorifics in both the grammar and lexicon of a language—so that they become continually invoked features during interaction—are likely to see the behavior of interaction and of social structure to be greatly shared and closely related. A clear example of this is provided by Geertz's (1960) fieldwork in Java. Javanese language speakers are confronted with three stylemes (levels of style) that are distinguished by a number of contrasting vocabulary items and by a set of high and low honorific terms that can be used to "raise" or "lower" speech half a level—in all, there is a repertoire encompassing six styles from which choices are to be made.

Javanese society is further characterized by sharp divisions among its three status groups. Which of the various styles is to be used among intimates, by an aristocrat to his/her social inferior, in government-related interactions, and so on is rigidly controlled. Although personal mood on the part of the speaker, the setting of any particular conversation, the topic being discussed, and other "contextual modifiers" may also influence the choice among styles to some degree, there is a certain givenness for how ranking distinctions are to be linguistically conveyed. In this manner, interaction making use of Javanese stylemes is controlled by social structural distinctions.

Groups for which status differentials are not known a priori, that is, low-context cultures, may exhibit a similarly close relationship between social order and linguistic features embedded in face-to-face conversation, although the direction of influence is likely to be reversed from the example above. In these cases, the interaction order seems to have a more powerful or primary influence on the social order than is true for the reverse. In a group that does not have a clear, a priori set of social-order–based considerations for ascertaining social status and social relationship of the interactants, there may be extensive utilization of partials shared with the interaction order in order to accomplish this (establish status and relationship). That is, definitions of social status, social identity, social responsibility, and so on are subject to interactional negotiation and construction. An example is provided above by Rosen's (1984) data on Sefrou, a small Moroccan town, in which actors can use the occasion of interaction, and the enquiries and topics established during interaction, in order to define and forge particular relationships and relationship-based obligations.

A given slot in interaction—the real-time production—is thus constrained by a number of behavioral orders (see figure 3–1).[7] The two research questions derived from this consideration become: Given a node in the flow of interaction, what interactional and social structural demands are placed on the tokens that can fill (realize) the slot? What are the differential consequences of the various options available and selected for the orders?

There are several possible abstract relationships and contraints to be explored. At particular moments, behavioral slots will be shown to be constrained by (1) the interaction order only; (2) the social order only; or (3) some combination or interaction of the interaction and social orders, in which there may be some precedence of application. Reciprocally, the moments of communication act as partials of (1) the interaction order; (2) the social order; or as partials (3a) simultaneously of the interaction and social orders; or (3b) sequentially of the interaction and social orders. (For an alternative formulation of the multiple constraints placed on rule-governed behavior, see Pearce and Cronen [1980:164]).

Configurations (1), (2) and (3a) are discussed extensively above; the fourth relationship, (3b), is probably the one needing the greatest explanation. I can conceive of a situation in which a slot is constrained, say, totally by the interaction

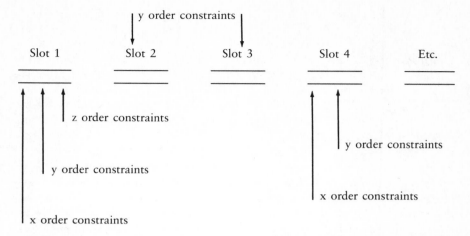

The figure indicates the sequential flow of single slots. Slot 1 is constrained by three orders. Slots 2 and 3 are constrained by only one order. Slot 4 is constrained by two orders. Not indicated on the diagram is the fact that there are multiple slots occurring simultaneously which are constrained to varying degrees by the three orders, and that there may be multiple constraints on a slot from any single order.

Figure 3–1. Interaction Slots and Constraints by Order

order. Imagine that there are three behavior units that can fill the slot (slot A). What this means is that *at the moment of production,* the three alternative interaction behaviors are in "free variation" with regard to the social order (Harris, 1951). There is no constraint coming from the social order which informs or regulates the selection among the three options. However, the ultimate and actual unit that is produced entails or implicates some subsequent behavioral choices "down the line" (slot B). These future behavioral selections may be multiply constrained by, and be multifunctional for, both the interaction and social orders. That is to say, the selection of the subsequent slot is drawn from a repertoire of options that is dependent on the previous interactionally based choices, and the selection of fillers for the subsequent slot is partially controlled by the social and interaction orders. In brief, the choice of A subsequently entails the choice of what can fill B, where A is conditioned by only one of the orders but B is conditioned by two. An alternate way of saying this is to suggest that the first unit invokes the realm of significances of one order, whereas the second unit invokes the realm of significances of two orders (see chapter 4 for further discussion on the notion of invocation).

Semiotic Order

There is a third order, the semiotic order, to be proposed here. The semiotic order contains partials of behavior directly related neither to social ranking and power differences among persons nor to the system sustaining focused and unfocused copresence.[8] Rather, it is concerned with the organization of multichannel behavior into units per se. The rules structuring information flow appropriate to particular channels of communication—or more accurately to what Birdwhistell (1970) labels infracommunication channels (kinesics, clothing, physical environment, and so on)—transcend particular interactional moments and social relationships and can be conceived of as comprising an order of communication in their own right. Particular information channels and/or modalities establish and are defined by constraints on expression, that is, constraints on what can possibly ("grammatically") be expressed, and, within the parameters of these constraints, on their employment by the remaining orders.

The Chomskyan (1965) notion of "competence" and Saussurian (1966) notion of "langue" represent attempts to study one contributing system of the semiotic order—the linguistic—in terms of its constituents and arrangements apart from their function in interaction or for the division of labor. Phonological constraints on sound combinations are another set of features belonging to the semiotic order. The study of design features for particular channels is also fundamental to the study of the semiotic order (cf. Hockett, 1958). For example, one feature of human language is that it enables "displaced speech" (Bloomfield, 1933) and is not rooted to the "immediacy of reference" (Pittenger, Hockett, and Danehy, 1960): speakers can refer to events, persons, objects, and so on that are not immediately sensible and are perhaps even imaginary. Gestural behavior, in contrast, seems more tied to the immediate situation of interaction, although some anaphoric reference or deixis is possible. Coulter writes in this regard:

> Of particular interest in the present chapter are the effects on the ontology of mind engendered by the use of verbal language. It may be proposed that each medium of human communication contains its own limitations and potentials for representation. For example, various media possess differing limitation over the range of vocabulary that they permit. As an instrument of communication, a violin allows a greater range of expression than a symbol; more distinctions may be drawn by sailors using a flashing light for communication than hoisted signal flags (each pattern of which denotes a single maneuver). Both music and dance are ideally designed for rendering narrative; the depiction of unfolding relations is far more difficult to accomplish with sculpture. And, the world-picture rendered by the photograph is likely to be more differentiated than one suggested by the painter. The choice of medium for relating to others can thus have significant implications for what the world is subsequently understood to be. (1985:117)

In general, there are semantic constraints and syntactic/structural constraints imposed by each order and by each channel within an order. There are "formal" constraints that seem to apply across all cultural applications of a particular medium (for example, Worth's [1975] suggestion that "pictures can't say ain't"), while there are also "substantive" constraints that represent a particular culture's organization of a particular channel (cf. Chomsky's [1968] different use of the terms *formal* and *substantive* with regard to language universals). The semiotic order establishes (1) the channels that are employed by particular groups and communities (cf. Hymes, 1974); (2) the units and unit relationships within and across channels (cf. McNeill, 1985); and (3) the semantic potential of each channel and its component units (cf. Mathiot, 1983).

This delineation of a separate semiotic order does not mean that the constituent semiotic units are not usable by the other orders. The semiotic order reverberates with the social and interaction orders when real-time interaction performances are generated and studied; in the abstract, however, it contains elements beyond either of the two orders, and, moreover, its organizing principles, its basis for structuring elements, are largely different from those of the other two. The interaction order provides a structure for face-to-face discourse; the social order for the social division of labor and responsibility; and the semiotic order, the grammar of particular channels of communication—indeed, as suggested above, the semiotic order defines what constitutes a channel for a particular group, organization, or society, for example, drum languages represented in one culture but not in another, so that it can be placed in the service of the other orders. All three orders make use of the same material (etic) behavior, yet how the behavior enters as a unit into each of the three orders is different (cf. Pike, 1967): (1) the interaction order makes use of an interactionally centered vocabulary for unitizing behavior; (2) the social order makes use of a rank- and power-based vocabulary, and is concerned with group structure and group processes such as recruitment and socialization; and (3) the semiotic order makes use of a structurally based vocabulary to describe the organization of the various channels (see table 3–1). To take one example, sounds may function as turn-requesting inhalations for the interaction order, as vocalic markers of ranking for the social order, and as phonemes for the semiotic order.

The multiple potentials for expression that each of the infracommunication channels of the semiotic order evidences can be differentially placed in the

Table 3–1
The Orders of Communication and Their Units

Interaction Order Units	Social Order Units	Semiotic Order Units
face formations	division of labor	chronemics
formulations	integration	haptics
greetings	recruitment	kinesics
terminations	resource distribution	olfactics
topic negotiation	socialization	proxemics
turn taking	status demarcation	vidistics

Note: The above is a partial listing of the constituent units and processes of each order.

service of the interaction and social orders. If intimacy can be expressed through both language and nonlanguage means, the interaction order may condition a different selection for the expression of this than does the social order.

In this manner, an order can be thought of as a set of interrelated resources (persons, objects, and so on) which are bound together—"ordered"—in some meaningful and coherent fashion. As noted, there are structural principles for the organization of elements within each order which are characteristic of each order. Nevertheless, each behavioral order stands only quasi-independently from the others. First, this stems partially from the multiple contributions that units of communication behavior make to the several orders. Second, to some degree the orders share functional requirements with each other. Each observation is described briefly below.

First, it should be pointed out that each of the various orders is not a singularly organized field. Within a single order, there are multiple levels, tracks, and hierarchies structuring the constituent units. When a behavior unit is seen to be a partial of, say, the interaction order, we must recognize that within this order it may relate to more than one of the component interaction (sub)systems or (sub)routines. That is to suggest that the unit of behavior may be a partial of multiple interaction systems constituting the interaction order: a unit of behavior might partially and differentially contribute to turn taking, topic negotiation, agenda establishment, and so on. Thus, in addition to multifunctionality of behavior across orders, there is multifunctionality across systems within each order.

Second, some of the functional requirements of the three orders may not be specific to a single order and may be shared to some degree across orders. The interaction and social orders, for example, can both be characterized by recruitment processes: the former allowing (or denying) persons' entry in and contributions to specific interactional events; the latter providing career trajectories for persons' attainment of, removal from, and movement toward specific social statuses. Both forms of recruitment concern the nature of access and membership, one examining access to the rights to establish or join ongoing interacting entities, the other examining access to the full array of socially defined positions. Particular interactional moments, such as gatekeeping encounters, may represent the intersection of both recruitment processes and may contain partials that define participants' rights and obligations in the immediate copresent event as well as over a longer duration. These partials include membership scheduling, transitions between and among positions, and training or cueing.

It is tempting to suggest that different terms be used to refer to communication participants depending on the order their behavior is being interpreted within at any given moment by the analyst. This would mean, for example, that *interactants* contribute behavioral partials to the interaction order, *(social) actors* or *personae*[9] to the social order, and *performers, speaker/hearers, producers,* and so on to the semiotic order. Some degree of consistency of usage is appropriate in this regard, although the multifunctional nature of behavioral contributions would also require some degree of flexibility and relativity; any one description of an individual qua *communicator* (the general category) is, of necessity, incomplete and nonabsolute.

During the course of one's behaving within the spatiotemporal boundaries of an interactional event, participants may focus on, or highlight, one or more of the constraining orders for their conduct, one or more of the orders to which they are actively contributing. Rather than suggest that there is only one primary order to which attention is to be paid—the interaction order—the present analytic scheme enables us to see that at various moments throughout the encounter, and sequentially during the encounter, the participants can and do orient to one, or some combination, of the different orders and hierarchies within each order.

That individuals orient to the different orders underlying their communication is demonstrated by data provided by Erickson and Schultz:

> In this instance, apparently, the student's hesitation was interpreted by the counselor merely as an indication of unfamiliarity with the sequencing and contextual cueing of conversational routines in the interview. But sometimes a hesitation had a social meaning with serious consequences for the interview as a whole. (1982:95)

As one illustration of this situation, a counselor might interpret a student's hesitation in discussing progress with current semester courses not simply as a temporary halt in the interactional flow, but as an implicit admission of poor school performance. Instead of repeating or clarifying the original question— responses aimed at, and belonging to, the interaction order—the counselor might decide to require additional coursework of the student and delay movement toward graduation—responses associated with the social order.

In brief, then, orders are likely to (1) contain units that are largely unique to each; (2) be guided for the most part by their own structuring principles; and (3) share some partials with each other (see figure 3–2). It should be reiterated here that a difference is being drawn between the study of information channels and the study of the functional orders that make use of these channels. The former is solely within the purview of the semiotic order, the latter of the social and interaction orders. Nevertheless, what is important to recognize is that *the proper study for social communication involves the multiple interdependencies between and among the various orders.* This explains Birdwhistell's (1970) insistence that the study of "nonverbal behavior" is only infracommunicationally centered; communication transpires through more than one behavioral channel and patterns both social and interactional functions. Birdwhistell writes, "Communication . . . appears to be a system which *makes use of* the channels of all sensory modalities" (1970:70; emphasis added).

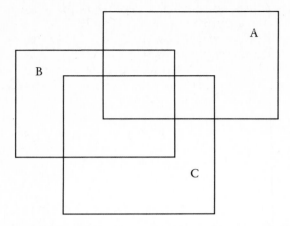

Each lettered box stands for one of the three orders of communication. The diagram indicates that each order has its own integral features as well as overlapping ones with the other orders.

Figure 3–2. Communication and the Three Orders

Communication presumes the existence of multichannel behavioral production but cannot be reduced to it. As Birdwhistell warns:

> The most comprehensive knowledge of linguistics and kinesics (*qua* linguistics and kinesics) will not permit us to analyze the precise social meaning of the content of an interactional sequence. On the other hand, we can, from the stream of audible sounds and the visible motions interchanged by the membership of the group, detect, isolate and describe the nature of the linguistic and kinesic behavior. (1970:97)

As Heilman adds, "Knowing all of the units or words of a particular language without knowing anything about the social conditions and contexts within which they are used does not make communication comprehensible" (1979:228). Social communication investigations must examine the structure of group membership and of social situations. In the terminology of the present chapter, communication can be understood only in the relationship among the interaction, social, and semiotic orders that constitute it, not by isolation of a single behavioral channel or order.[10]

It is for these reasons that I have suggested the relevance of ethnographic and contextual studies of discourse (see chapter 2; also Sigman, 1983a, 1985a). Communication researchers—and emergently, social communication researchers—need to look at the meaning of discourse units as these units relate to orders other than the one concerned primarily with the punctiform present or local nature of the interaction. Not only do we need to locate the units in the immediate event, but we must consider the event itself to be a unit comprised of subunits (the discourse units) which can be located in larger structures.

Summary and Revised Definition of Communication

To summarize the discussion up to this point, then, Goffman is largely correct in suggesting that there is a separable organization to interaction, much as language can be seen to have a grammar analytically apart from, although clearly influenced by and closely related to, social use and context (cf. Bloomfield, 1933; Chomsky, 1965). This separable organization can and must be distinguished as part of the general research program for communication study. However, while abstracting a code (or codes) of interaction is thus feasible and productive (see Schenkein, 1978; Stubbs, 1983), this enterprise potentially fails to uncover the complex, interrelated, and multiple constraints on behavior observable during actual moments of interaction. The interaction order, which is organized in terms of units and unit relationships of its own, shares in its actual production partials with both the social and semiotic orders. It is the relationship among the interaction, social, and semiotic orders which is the peculiar concern of social communication.

Communication is isomorphic with neither the interaction, the social, nor the semiotic order. Communication comprises information flow or meanings related to the interaction, social, and semiotic orders. As a continuous, multiple-channel social process, it regulates, and, in turn, is contributed to, by behavior from multiple orders. Communication is comprised of interrelated and multiply regulated partials, which can be seen to constitute completely a single order only when they are considered in narrow analytic isolation. This definition informs, and elaborates upon, the focus in chapter 2 on studying units of communication that serve to construct both interactional events and social relationships.

Communication can be defined as the continuous process of information generation and storage which constitutes the behavior of a social group and which represents the integration of the three orders discussed in this chapter. Communication is constituted and contributed to by the three orders. It is the unique integrity of the interactions and interdependencies of the three orders, and their multifunctional sharing and patterning of units, which sets communication apart from any of the three orders in isolation from the others. Communication is the continuous process of information flow that is comprised of interaction-, social-, and semiotic-related messages.

This definition in no way dissolves the earlier argument for the sui generis status of communication (see chapter 1). Communication, as social information flow, can be studied with regard to the three behavioral orders that constitute it, but the three orders and the emerging communication process are not reducible to the persons who seem to act upon, and react to, each other under apparently localized conditions. Individual roles within the communication process, and individual social identities and personalities, are the products of participants' exposure to particular facets of the interaction, social, and semiotic orders, not the initiating points for society, interaction, or infracommunication channel organization.

Notes

1. Birdwhistell (1970) aligns cultural analysis with a from-above approach to data, and communicational analysis with a from-below one. As I use the terms here, *from-above* and *from-below* approaches are integrated in social communication research, although the former is emphasized.

2. Aspects of this position are criticized by other sociologists. While otherwise laudatory toward Goffman's work, Giddens criticizes Goffman for his individualistic and intentionalistic stance: "Goffman's analyses of encounters presume motivated agents rather than investigating the sources of human motivation." (1984:70).

3. My reading of Goffman, admittedly critical, leads me to think that some of the interesting interaction effects, and intimate coeffects of the interaction and social orders, are overlooked and treated glibly by him (for example, Goffman, 1983a:6, 17). There is a greater mixture between the two than admitted by Goffman. However, this chapter does not address the issue of how consistently Goffman's work over the years can be seen to adhere to the separation of an interaction order.

4. The relationship between social organizational distinctions and processes and their symbolic (behavioral) realizations is not easily characterized as one-to-one either. I recently received a letter from my dean with "Professor Sigman" typed as the salutation but crossed out and replaced by a handwritten "Stuart." The co-occurrence between the communication mode (for example, typed versus handwritten) and address terminology (title-plus-last-name versus first-name) is interesting. This gives rise to a multifunctional albeit subtle message. Apparently, it was felt that *two* terms were needed to characterize a single social structural arrangement; the two terms placed in opposition to each other yet joined together ambiguously capture the multifaceted relationship between a dean and one of his/her faculty members.

5. Goffman defines social order as "the consequence of any set of moral norms that regulates the way in which persons pursue objectives" (1963:8). Social order is thus for Goffman a general category, which includes interaction, economic, and legal orders (cf. Leeds-Hurwitz, 1986). In the present context I use the term not to refer to the general class, but rather as one of the substantive categories subordinate to the general class, equal in level, specificity, and scope to the interaction order. Social order refers to rankings of persons and distribution of task responsibilities.

6. The study of alternative health-care delivery systems indicates the extent to which it is American middle-class conceptions that are coincident with the boundary features of the doctor-patient interaction (for example, continuity of care with the same doctor, limited access hours, availability in office but not at home, cocktail party, shopping center). See the chapters in Harwood (1981).

7. This is a simplified example, since I assume here that the initial slots derive from the interaction order. It is also conceivable for the appearance of slots to derive from the social order and for such slots to be sensitive to subsequent interaction order constraints. Empirical work in this area is clearly called for.

8. In thinking about the interaction order, it is necessary that this be broadened to include interactional engagements between and among society members who are not in each other's physical presence. For example, there are rules for periods of withdrawal and absence. Similarly, the social order makes use of elements that may be noncopresently displayed, as in the case of relationship continuity signals, for example, a wedding band worn even when the partners are not in each other's presence.

9. See Geertz's (1975) distinction between "dramatis personae" and "actors" as relevant to Balinese constructions of self.

10. This delimitation can be used to establish communication as a scholarly discipline distinct from either linguistics or social psychology proper. I have heard many stories in the last few years in which the viability and academic integrity of departments of communication were being questioned by university central administrators. The above delimitation may prove a welcome arsenal in the argument supporting the continuation of separate departments. Social communication is not adequately studied within either linguistics or social psychology. It should be noted, however, that I do not consider interpersonal cummunication to be a level of communication (and hence a domain of investigation) separate from social communication. All of communication is social. Interpersonal communication is what is seen when the analyst limits his/her observations to copresent moments and messages, without examining multiorder, multiepisode patterns and functions.

4
Multifunctional Communication as Invocation

Invocation and Entailment

The present articulation of a social approach to communication theory suggests that individuals do not behave simply according to rules or rule selections. Rather, their behavioral selections appear to be guided by, and to invoke, a more encompassing and more general social-semiotic code (see Halliday, 1978). This larger code contains nonequivalently valenced options for behaving and is differentially distributed to, and accessed by, members of the community or group.

The emphasis throughout this book on the concept of invocation represents an attempt to provide some analytic means for systematically referencing particular, moment-by-moment interactional events and rule selections to the more encompassing behavior pattern (or patterns). The act of behaving—more concretely, of behaving in a particular way in a particular episode—serves to invoke the larger streams (contexts) in which that act fits and is meaningful. Multiple coding systems constrain and facilitate behavioral production at any given moment, and while conversation and interaction analyses have focused on the most "immediate," "visible," or "local" constraints, social communication advocates examination of the multiple ("immediate" and "distal") mutually influencing constraints and contexts (see chapters 1 and 2).

The act of behaving in a particular way, and of not behaving in some other ways, serves to invoke a set of relevance structures (Schutz and Luckmann, 1973), contexts (Bateson, 1972), programs (Scheflen, 1968), and/or frames (Goffman, 1974), and to negate or deny the applicability of others. At the moment of production, behavior units and unit combinations call into operation (or resonate with) some selected set from the numerous hierarchical structures that "could" govern the behavior. The specific set of invoked codes or structures serves to contextualize and provide the meaningfulness of the behavior produced. The relationship is, of course, reciprocal, for the particular act being performed simultaneously (1) brings into focus the larger context and code transpiring in and relevant at that moment of action, and (2) is itself brought into some meaningful focus by the larger context and code from which its identity is inseparable (see Pike, 1967).

As described in chapter 2, discrete interactional events—discrete from the point of view of the actors' socially patterned terminology for describing communication events or the researcher's observational time frame (cf. Erickson and Shultz, 1981)—are partial units contributing to, and constrained by, a larger stream of continuous multichannel behavior.[1] In this light, students of social communication are trained to study neither the isolated episode nor the single behavioral code, but rather the two in relationship to each other, as this relationship comprises and governs the larger stream. More specifically, social communication researchers study (1) isolated episodes as they inform us about, and are multiply related to, the codes of the interaction, social, and semiotic orders; and (2) the place and function of these episodes in the larger multiorder and multichannel stream called *communication.*

Invocation is intended as a neutral term with regard to an actor's consciousness of his/her behvioral performance(s). Consciousness and intentionality are themselves social constructions, and, as suggested in chapter 1, particular moments of consciousness and intentionality are only partial units or moments regulated by the larger, continuous communication stream (cf. Gergen and Davis, 1985). This larger stream defines and patterns moments of acceptable (and unacceptable) self-awareness and self-monitoring during behavioral production. Wilden remarks that "in the last analysis . . . , it is not really of great significance what anyone *intends* or *means;* in the end it is what they *say* and *do* that counts" (1979:25; emphasis in original). Thus, the notion of invocation is a statement about the relationship of an act (unit) to some level or levels (context) of the larger stream, not about the relationship between an actor and his/her acts. In this regard, it is similar to Birdwhistell's (1970) suggestion that behavior units in conjunction with each other signal or cross-reference the contexts that provide for their meaningfulness and predictability.

Social actors are unable to verbalize about the multiple invocation potentials of their behavior in most cases. Therefore, multifunctional communication analyses require long-term ethnographic exposure to and familiarity with the "field" so that the observer can examine the multiple antecedent and consequent features of observable behavior (cf. Corsaro, 1982). The goal is to interpret a behavior's multifunctionality, that is, its situatedness in multiple orders, levels, and hierarchies.

Moreover, social actors do not have equal access to, and command of, the various codes and subsidiary codes sustaining the larger, continuous stream (cf. Hymes, 1974; Bernstein, 1975; Halliday, 1978). Two interactants can, for example, perform the "same" behavior derived from the "same" rule, yet the *significance* of their invocations—when related by an analyst back to each individual's position within the social order and to his/her access to the attendant behavioral codes—need not be equivalent. Wilden writes:

A code or set of codes is the basis of the creative principle that makes messages and relationships *possible* in the first place, at the same time as the constraints embodied in a code make an even greater variety of qualitatively different messages and relationships *impossible* in the system as it stands. (1979:15; emphasis in original)

Depending on each participant's complete behavioral repertoire, that is, his/her totality of available codes, there exist different configurations of possible and impossible messages. These different configurations provide contrasting scaffoldings upon which particular message productions are placed.

Consider the following hypothetical example. Say that actor A has group-sanctioned access to and command of $code_1$, $code_2$, and $code_3$. His/her momentary production of a behavior governed by the rules of $code_1$ will be "marked" (Hymes, 1974), in that it represents a partial selection (whether conscious or not) of a $code_1$ unit, and not one of $code_2$ or $code_3$. The "meaning" of the unit is constituted, at least in part, by its general placement and function within $code_1$, and by its status as a particular selection from the individual's total array of codes (cf. de Saussure, 1966). For actor B, on the other hand, who commands a more limited repertoire, say, $code_1$ alone, the performance of the physically (and even referentially) similar behavior from this code is differentially meaningful. One aspect of this contrasting meaning results from the fact that the performance represents the "only" behavior available to this actor at the moment—what Giddens refers to as "the margins of what can count as action" (1984:14) for that person—and is an instantiation and "reminder" of the actor's limited social experiences and options.[2] (By implication, it may also serve as an instantiation and reminder of the limited social experiences and options typically accorded to, encountered by, and expected of the individual's fellow group members.) The "same" behavior units—from the etic standpoint (Pike, 1967)—can invoke qualitatively distinct contexts or interpretation frameworks, especially when there are varying repertoires of behaviors and codes from which selections are permissibly made. In brief, as de Saussure notes (1966), an item is meaningful, in part, in relation to what else *could* have been chosen but was not.

As outlined above, it is the continuous stream of message-production moments as this invokes and articulates the more encompassing set of message options, that is, the totality of individual code repertoires and of patterns of differential access to these repertoires, which is the object of social communication study. This is to suggest that social communication research is less concerned with the rules that govern conduct for any particular context, situation, or activity, than with the multiple rules, group membership requirements, and access patterns across multiple contexts, situations, and/or activities. Rather than study singular behavioral rules, social communication theory is interested in the ideas about people and events—the definition and nature of being a person in that group—which are revealed by the rules. Winch writes, "A man's social relations with his fellows are permeated with his ideas about reality. Indeed, 'permeated' is hardly a strong enough word: social relations are expressions of ideas about reality" (1958:23). This description is consistent with the discussion in chapter 3, in which social communication theory is seen to emphasize the interrelations of behavior derived from and structured by the interaction, social, and semiotic orders.

There are thus four interrelated features of communication for investigation: (1) there are message production moments and locations, for example, what have variously been labeled "communication events" and "episodes" (cf. Hymes, 1974; Frentz and Farrell, 1976; Gumperz, 1982); (2) there are the abstract behavioral codes and specifications for option selections; (3) there is an articulatory relationship between (1) and (2) during actual and particular moments of interaction; and (4) there are multifunctional, and especially ideological, implications of (1), (2), and (3). It should be noted that I have reversed the usual order of code (2) and production (1). Although it is true that the code precedes production in a historical sense, the former can be empirically revealed only via the latter. Further, as elaborated below, the two cannot be described except in relation to each other.

Performances, that is, the actual moments of behavioral production, are not seen here as bastardized or incomplete realizations of some underlying code (or codes), for they require the code as a basis for founding comprehension, meaning, and predictability (cf. Chomsky, 1965, 1968). Performances are actions that bring to completion (invoke) at particular moments different aspects of reality as governed by abstract communication codes (socially patterned rules and values). Turner defines performance thus: "The term 'performance' is, of course, derived from Old English *parfournir*, literally, 'to furnish completely or thoroughly.' To perform is thus to bring something about, to consummate something, or to 'carry out' a play, order, or project" (1980:160). Adapting Turner's approach, Pacanowsky and O'Donnell-Trujillo write, "Performances are not inauthentic nor [sic] superficial; they are the very things which bring to completion a sense of reality" (1983:131). Moreover, it is not a background of "potential" meaning which is at issue when codes are performed, for the act of performance serves to commit the actor (as well as copresent and absent others) to a particular set or particular sets of behavioral codes (cf. Giddens, 1984). This is accomplished even though not every option—for example, for units, entailments, and so on—is actually performed on any one occasion. As noted above, the performance invokes, realizes, or brings into play the larger code (or one of its subsidiary codes); it places it into the center or foreground of the interactional arena.

Invocation functions along a conservative track by reproducing and reaffirming existing behavioral codes and forms (cf. Giddens, 1984). Simmel (1898) provides an example concerning moral codes. He writes, "In preserving his own honor, the individual preserves at the same time the honor of his own social circle" (1898:682). Honor and behavior that is honorable are socially defined and regulated. To act honorably, it is necessary for a person to bestow and to have bestowed on him/herself a particular label and status; these various actions taken together affirm the applicability and rightness of the social-cultural codes regarding honor and its constitution (cf. Archer, 1982). Invocation thus represents the calling into reference or relevance of a particular order or set of hierarchical levels during performance.

Entailment emerges as follows: As the result of the invocation of a particular level or order, certain behavioral choices are likely to be entailed or implicated for that single actor and/or all others in the scene for subsequent performance. Invoking a set of meanings at time-$_1$ entails related selections at time-$_2$ (cf. Ervin-Tripp, 1972). The entailment may concern different behavior units within a single hierarchy or order, or across hierarchies and orders. The entailments are not personally or individually generated, however, but rather are typically found to be part of the socially organized code. That is to suggest, the code itself specifies entailment relationships among selections within levels, hierarchies, and orders, as well as across these.

Entailment can be seen as a feature of the multiple invocation potential of behavior. For example, to invoke a name for someone in the Moroccan city of Sefrou is to (1) place attributes on him/her; (2) characterize the interactional situation of application; and (3) establish one's own identity and connections to the named person (see Rosen, 1984). In other words, there is multilevel work performed by the invocation, and, as a result, multiple behavioral consequences are entailed for all parties involved. Individuals may on occasion seek to subvert certain established entailments (see the discussion below on Goldschmidt's [1972] example of a woman's choice of burial site for her infant and what it was supposed to entail with regard to her marital status). Nevertheless, and in general, behavioral selections within the interaction, social, or semiotic order entail, and, therefore, constrain choices and meanings for the remaining orders.

Invocation and entailment do not mean, however, that a performance is necessarily a precise duplicate of the behavioral code(s) in their entirety. As noted above, codes generally contain multiple options and entailments, whereas a performance presumably is seen (and heard, smelled, and so on) to comprise particular selections from the unit options and the alternate branchings. In this manner, articulation represents the particular confrontation or relationship between the actual, lived, performed behavior and the code associated with the order or hierarchical level being invoked at that time. Articulation refers to the nature and quality of the adherence of the performed behavior to the code. There are several articulatory relationships between codes and performances, among these negotiation, calibration, adumbration, contradiction, denouncement, and acquiescence. (See Berger [1984] for a list that shows how semiotic signs can be modified in varying ways.) Goffman shrewdly points to the multiple potential articulatory relationships between action and expected norms in this way:

> Motive for adhering to a set of arrangements need tell us nothing about the effect of doing so. Effective cooperation in maintaining expectations implies neither belief in the legitimacy or justice of abiding by a convention contract in general . . . , *nor* personal belief in the ultimate value of the particular norms that are involved. Individuals go along with current interaction arrangements for a wide variety of reasons. (1983b:5; emphasis in original)

Metacommunicational signals (Bateson, 1972), contextualization cues (Gumperz, 1982), and rekeyings (Goffman, 1974) serve to invoke qualitatively distinct hierarchies and frameworks for behavior, and so facilitate the multiple articulations of behavior and code.

Goldschmidt's (1972) attempt to develop an "ethnography of encounters" can be seen to provide data, derived from fieldwork in Uganda, on the articulatory relationship between observable behavior and invoked codes. In the following extract from the analysis, a young girl in her late teens is confronted by the obligation to make funeral arrangements for her dead infant, born to her and her lover, yet she also recognizes that the decision as to burial location may entail acquiescence to a marriage arranged on her behalf by her father to someone other than the child's father:

> Finally, her manner of forcing the issue is itself significant. The issue clearly at stake is not the burial of the child, but the marriage to Chepkongo. She is aware that her acquiescence in the burial will force an acceptance of the marriage. She uses her fearlessness of the spirits as a weapon with which to bring these powerful men to heel. It is her cultural callousness, her disengagement from the "normal" Sebei fears, that enables her to act thus. This is not a denial of culture. Rather, Yeya *uses* her culture, rather than submitting to it; her act would be meaningless contrary to accepted standards of conduct and sentiment, to which those around her do submit. (1972:63; emphasis in original)

Summarizing a related case, Goldschmidt writes:

> In the rhetoric of the argumentation, we find that (as with Yeya) the protagonists use the culture for their own ends, rather than merely being used by it. They accuse one another of witchcraft and make other insinuations regarding one another's behavior. Clearly, they are not burdened by their beliefs—which is not to say they are unbelieving. (1972:66)

Weick provides an interesting notion that highly rigid codes of behavior may result in what might be considered disarticulations:

High formalization, consisting of a rule for everything and procedure manuals that are three inches thick rather than one-quarter inch thick, may mean that there is more threat to freedom and more reactance, more learned helplessness, more sabotage, more energy devoted to bypassing formal constraints. Formalization predicts performance, but its effects are mediated by predictable responses from streetwise human actors. (1983:20).

Action ostensibly designed by participants to sabotage or bypass otherwise accepted and expected conduct establishes a relevance (and irrelevance) and applicability (and nonapplicability) of the invoked rules. The articulatory relationship—in this case, rejection—is real and evident, albeit negative.

The reflexive nature of articulation and code can give rise to (1) reproduction, and/or (2) change of the code. In cases where articulatory relationships do not question the rules or their applicability, they can nevertheless be seen to provide metacommunication on them. In particular, the applicability of the behavior in the specified context is affirmed in a fairly "straightforward" manner. In other cases, articulation gives rise to rule changes over time. As Cronen, Pearce, and Tomm write, "The relationship between structure [invoked codes] and action [performed behavior] is reflexive. Structure emerges from patterns of coordinated action and turns back upon those patterns guiding them" (1985:205). There is a reflexive nature here such that new patterns can emerge from the articulation and confrontation of the code and the performance. Turner writes in this regard, "The rules may frame the performance, but the flow of action and interaction within that frame may conduce to hitherto unprecedented insights and even generate new symbols and meanings, which may be incorporated into subsequent performances" (1980:160). I have previously described one aspect of this process under the rubric "discourse rehearsal" (see Sigman and Donnellon, in press), in which participants adhere to preexisting rules yet simultaneously create novel applications for them.

As noted, one additional question encouraged by the social communication framework concerns the sociopolitical implications (entailments) of particular rule invocations and distributional patterns. The work of the British "critical linguists" represents one contribution to this research stream (cf. Fowler, Hodge, Kress, and Trew, 1979). My reading of the "organizational culture" literature leads me to conclude that it has strong potential for a similar contribution (cf. Putnam and Pacanowsky, 1983).

Rather than study rules specific to a single behavior or activity, one focus of social communication theory is the ideas about people and events that are revealed in, and exemplified by, the multiple communication rules constituting the social communication repertoire. As Bateson writes:

I classify together the simplest conventions of communication and the most abstract cultural and psychiatric premises, and insist that a vast range of premises of this sort are implicit in every message. For example, if I believe that the world is "agin" me and I am in communication with some other person, the premise about the world being "agin" me is going to be built into the way in which I structure my messages and interpret his. In a sense, a philosophy of life is describable as a set of rules for constructing messages, and the individual's culture or *Weltanschauung*, call it what you will, is built into his conventions of communication. (Bateson, 1953:2)

And as Shweder and Miller write: "The way individuals perceive, describe, and explain each other's behavior is decisively influenced by received conceptualizations of the person in relationship to the moral-social order and the natural order" (1985:56).

Briefly, interaction and/or other behavior partials are multifunctional: they can operate at multiple levels within a single hierarchy, and they can be shared by, or represent the intersection of, two or more hierarchies. Moreover, behavior partials can be seen as *context and code invocation signals,* markers of the hierarchical streams invoked at particular moments and entailed for subsequent moments.

In light of this discussion, it is possible to explore the multiple invocation possibilities of human social conduct. The remainder of this chapter does so with reference to a specific set of empirical data that have been extensively published elsewhere (Sigman, 1982, 1984, 1985b, 1985/86, 1986) but not adequately discussed with regard to this aspect of social communication.

Recruitment Partials

The question the data were collected to address concerns the mechanism(s) by which social groups provide for their continuity in the face of the death, retirement, or incapacity of their "personnel," or members. As Harré (1979) observes, biology does not set the limits of culture, but it provides problems to which cultures must find solutions. Social recruitment is thus studied as a process that functions to organize group continuity and survival by ensuring and patterning the availability of persons appropriate to the particular positions and relationships constitutive of the group. As anthropologists and sociologists generally note, the individual (biological) organism and the social structure (social order) are not analytically simultaneous (see Linton, 1936, 1940, 1942; Durkheim, 1938; Sorokin, 1947): the existence of a position or status within the latter can be conceptually distinguished from the particular person or persons filling each "slot." Yet the persistence of the social group as an integral whole and of any one constituent position is predicated on the capacity of the group or society to provide (continually) for the replenishment of each available position. This is an ideal-type working assumption, since it can be observed that at particular points in history, socially defined positions may disappear or go unfilled, their definitions may be changed, and so on.

Nevertheless, recruitment can be seen as a separable and patterned system of behavior serving to admit individuals into group membership and to provide options (or requirements) for them to fill (or be prepared to fill) relevant social positions. It represents a multiparticipant and mutichannel system by which individuals are moved into filling statuses within a structure, and/or by which gatekeeping vis-à-vis these individuals is accomplished (cf. Erickson and Shultz, 1982). Putnam writes, "Recruitment entails power and control—the unobtrusive control of selection and training and the power relationships that benefit from these activities" (1983:50). In this respect, an analysis of recruitment recognizes the existence of socially defined and regulated trajectories, careers, or biographies (Goffman, 1961a; Glaser and Strauss, 1971): the processes by which individuals "volunteer," are "forced," and/or are provided with options to move from one social position to another, or by which they are expected to engage in such transitions, or by which provisions are made for them to do so, or by which barricades to these opportunities are created, are neither random nor idiosyncratically determined.

Social recruitment is not a unitary process, but is rather comprised of a variety of partials. In addition to the transition rituals that accomplish and symbolize movement between and among statuses, there exist procedures for selecting individuals to assume relevant social positions, that is, to undergo status passage, as well as procedures for blocking mobility (cf. van Gennep, 1960; Glaser and Strauss, 1971). Thus, recruitment involves evaluation procedures in which individuals' fitness—skill, acumen, attitude, knowledge, appearance, and so on—for particular positions is tested. Initial assignments and/or subsequent transitions to the various positions constitutive of the social order, as well as exits from the particular system altogether, may be based on the evaluative interactions. A mythology may exist which justifies, establishes selection criteria for, and regulates particular assignment and reassignment decisions and outcomes—especially explanations for "success" and "failure"—and the total array of movement patterns (cf. Becker and Strauss, 1956; Goffman, 1961a). The patterning of these partials enables social groups to fill social positions made available for whatever reasons in a continuous and organized fashion.

Two skilled-care nursing facilities located near Philadelphia were studied ethnographically to shed light on social recruitment. At the start of the research, the two facilities, People's Home and Sisters of Faith Home,[3] were judged to be social institutions confronting the necessity of establishing, maintaining, and carrying out some recruitment procedures; it was assumed that in order to survive, each had to fill vacant residential positions (operationalized in the form of a bed in a ward) occasioned by residents' deaths, discharges, and/or transfers to different positions. As described below, the definitions of the positions at the two facilities were not equivalent semiotically, and in conjunction with this nonequivalence, the recruitment procedures and partials differed.

People's Home

People's Home (PH) was operated as a private and profit-making facility. In apparent consequence of the profit orientation, the directors of this facility aimed at making the home maximally appealing to its various clients (actual and potential). Both the owner and the chief administrator of PH told me that private nursing homes, by providing a physically appealing building that attracted a variety of types of "customers," were able to maintain some competitive edge over other geriatric facilities. The various People's Home programs aimed at improvement and expansion of the physical plant were designed with the idea of expanding the range of potential applicants. The owner and the administrator agreed that private nursing facilities draw applicants from a pool of individuals who seek particular services and special facilities for relatives to be institutionalized. Sam Applebaum, the owner, suggested, "Private nursing homes have got to be competitive; these [sic] must offer the facility in order to attract customers."

At PH, the satisfaction of these presumed customer demands was seen to entail the implementation and employment of a ward system that provided the different physical locations of the facility with differing definitions—that is, assessments of patients' behavioral predictability. Each section of People's Home was designated by the administration as appropriate for a different category of patient (see figure 4–1). The segregation of patients was one of the selling

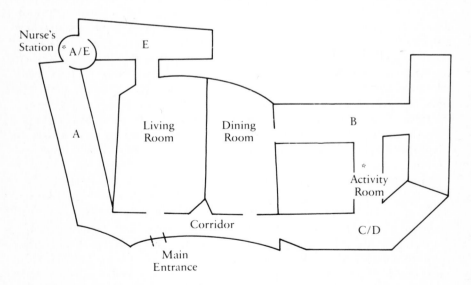

Not drawn to scale; certain features obscured.

Figure 4–1. Layout of People's Home

points from the administrative perspective. This segregation presumedly enabled each patient to commingle with selected peers and to receive treatment from health professionals who specialized or at least had prior experience in caring for particular types of patients. Some of the residents and their families, when interviewed about the decision to apply to PH, referred to the nursing home as primarily a place for meeting and socializing with other people, that is, as a residential community. The fact that it was a skilled facility received secondary attention.

(Conversation between Mrs. Lutz and Tony, two PH residents):
Mrs. Lutz at one point says: Yeah. My doctor said he didn't want me being alone, there should be other people for me. My daughter looked around, and she said this is the best one she thinks. There are people, I like it.

(Discussion in dining room with a new patient, Mrs. Fogel):
Fogel: My family did this. I don't know why I'm here.
SJS: Maybe they want you to rest?
Fogel: Why? I'm not tired. Dopey me, I gave my sister power of attorney. I couldn't figure out why at first. Now I know. Tell me, how do you reverse the power of attorney? I guess I need a lawyer, right?
SJS: I don't know.
Fogel: I still tell you, it's still better than sitting all alone at home, by yourself. It's a wonderful place here. I wish they'd get me out. I don't know, maybe I'll adjust. There's still nothing like your own home. I guess it could be worse. I have my own, a duplex; I've got a tenant.

Residents of PH spoke about sociability and the desire to be among people as their primary reasons for entering the facility; medical needs, while not inconsequential, were taken as given and as secondary to the desire not to live alone.

Several factors seemed to account for the administrator's decision to accept or reject an applicant to People's Home: (1) the availability of family funds, (2) the total number and the classification of beds available at the time of the application, and (3) the type of patient. Applications to the facility were considered by the administrator only when there was an existing (rather than an anticipated) bed vacancy and when the preliminary descriptions of the applicant-patient provided by physicians, social workers, and/or family members indicated that the individual was suitable for that open position. When a specific bed became available at the home, the first individual to apply *at that time* who was considered appropriate for occupancy of the bed was accepted. The facility did not maintain, or feel the obligation or need to maintain, a waiting list. Thus, potential residents were allowed entry into the facility only when an apparent match existed between patient characteristics and the available section space(s).

Nonadherences to this apparent rule were generally observed to be the result of a low population census and of the need, expressed by the administrator, to fill some of the empty beds. These deviations from an otherwise rigid ward system—which can be seen as an intrusion of economic considerations on the interaction order and on social relational aspects of the social order—and the language used to justify them, are described in more detail below.

An individual might enter PH through any one of the four residential sections; however, the initial slots were not equivalent.[4] Each section of the facility was designed for a different category or type of patient. As noted above, such a ward system was justified on the basis of the need to attract the full spectrum of geriatric patients to People's Home. As a result, there was differential access to and entry on each ward. "Confused" and "disoriented" patients (as labeled by the institution) were assigned to A or C/D sections because of the high staff-patient ratios there, as compared to the ratios on E and B. E and B were reserved primarily for "alert" patients. The varying staff-patient ratios were said to be a response to the differing health and supervisory needs of the various patients at PH.

In addition to this, the physical plant differed among the various sections: A, C/D, and portions of B had linoleum floors, which were considered easier to maintain with incontinent residents than the carpets found on E. There appeared to be more attention paid to aesthetic details (for example, matching wallpaper, signed and numbered lithographs) on E section and on portions of B section. In brief, the physical environment as a message or information construction (statement) reflected and reinforced divisions made within the social order.

In some respects, the most important aspect of the patient-to-section match was concerned with the potential newcomer's capacity to contribute to and benefit from social life—especially contact with one's peers—on the particular section assigned to him/her. Assignment to a particular section of the home entailed the most likely social group(s) that the new patient would be allowed, encouraged, or expected to join. In other words, each slotting decision invoked and belonged to the system of friendship formation and, as described below, of patient identity construction, in addition to the system of recruitment (assignment). Patients who entered People's Home entered a facility with clearly defined, delimited, and differentiated wards, and placement on one of the wards entailed specific expectations for the patient's career at the facility. This is consistent with the view of Strauss et al. concerning the relationship between diagnoses and ecological/ward definitions in psychiatric hospitals: "Health is not only a condition, it is related to spatial location. Its location is determined, for the most part, by conceptions of ward shape and hospital ecology" (Strauss, Schatzman, Bucher, Ehrlich, and Sabshin, 1964:112).

The criterion of matching incoming patients and available beds (and wards) was consistent with the combined definition of People's Home as a skilled nursing facility and a residential community. Staff members recognized that each of the four sections promoted and was guided by different rules for social interaction and peer contact. Moreover, there existed few opportunities and sanctions for extended interward interaction to develop; friendship among the residents was predicated on the staff members' assumption that individuals must be allowed to reside and associate with patients of a similar type. This attitude was, in general, accepted and reinforced by the residents themselves—and their family members (see below)—who avoided conversation and other activities with residents not from their own section in such places as the living room and the dining room. In addition to this, residents adhered to certain tacit spatial allocations. They avoided entering territories (wards) outside their own sections, apparently in order not to come in contact with the patients there.

It should be noted that B had a somewhat ambiguous status within the overall array of wards available for patient assignments. Consider the following statement from the social services director:

Carol: There's a big difference in the patients. Activities we can do on A or C/D, or they're interested in [doing], we can't get away with on E or B. Actually, B is difficult to describe. B is, you have some very fine women there; they'd get along with Mrs. Bergman and the others at E. Of course, we don't have room for them. But then you have some which are just, well, they're like our A or C/D, and you've seen what they're like.

There were several influences on this ambiguous and transitional definition of B. First, although B was only a few years older than E, it showed its age by no longer being attractive to the "best customers." Newer alert patients and their families were likely to prefer E for the initial residential section—ostensibly because of its clientele, decor, and ambience—even though B was also intended for such residents. In addition to this, as it was opened before E, B had a slightly older population, one that had been institutionalized for a longer period of time and therefore was more prone to debilitating illnesses. This made it increasingly difficult for the administrator to persuade incoming alert patients to take up residence there. The final aspect of this cycle is that the increasing availability of E for alert patients meant that the role of B was modified to handle overflow from A and C/D.[5]

The nonequivalence of the residential sections which influenced initial slotting decisions by the administrator could also be seen to shape transfer procedures at People's Home. Staff members initiated reassignments when a patient was no longer considered suitable for his/her current ward placement. Change was usually viewed by the staff in terms of patient deterioration; there was little assumption that nursing home patients ever improve. (See the geriatric literature, for example, Markson [1971], which indicates that nursing homes are often viewed as places in which to die.) The ostensible aim of a transfer was to select a section of the facility which matched the patient's then current medical condition or functioning level. As a result, the general flow of reassigned patients was from the most prestigious sections to lesser evaluated ones in the home (see table 4–1).

Several variations on this general theme of reassigning deteriorated patients can be noted. In some cases, assessments (reassessments) of a patient's medical-psychological condition occurred immediately upon the patient's entry into the facility. Transfers based on this criterion were likely when a major discrepancy existed between the staff members' evaluations of the incoming patient and the family members' and/or professionals' original reports. However, the majority of transfers were initiated for long-term residents of the facility who were judged unqualified for their existing assignments.[6] It is interesting to note the participants involved in these patient judgments: Although a staff committee existed at PH for monitoring patients' medical conditions and behavior performances and for regulating transfers (the Health Care Review Team), evaluations of patient inappropriateness were also made by the residents' section peers. In a sense, older patients could be seen "auditioning" newcomers. The residents gained information about their peers through observation of and interaction with them; these encounters enabled the veteran residents to determine future response patterns. In addition, relatives of the residents could be observed encouraging particular treatment procedures for residents, for both their own family members residing at PH and the latter's roommates (real and potential). Relatives outside the facility were apparently acutely aware of the status and prestige system (the social order) within PH, specifically, how the resident's prestige was dependent upon that accorded his/her section mates. Therefore, relatives negotiated with the administration of the facility for a particular status and residential placement, by encouraging placements, involvement in activities, and so on for their own family members; by encouraging particular transfers for other patients; or by rejecting potential roommates.

Table 4–1
People's Home Transfers

To:	From:			
	A	B	C/D	E(A/E)
A	0	4	1	3
B	0	4	1	1
C/D	3	3	1	0
E(A/E)	0	0	0	0

Source: These data are based on archival and/or observational records for September 2, 1980, to June 16, 1981.
Same-ward transfers = 5 (24% of total transfers)
Different-ward transfers = 16 (76%)

As noted, economic pressures and applicant profiles on occasion prompted the administrator to accede to what were otherwise considered "inappropriate placements." These decisions, many of which were made to satisfy family members, need not be considered strictly as deviations from an ideal, for they were managed by the administrator and her staff in a manner that appeared still to invoke and articulate the prevailing social order code. Buttny writes in this respect, "The use of corrective mechanisms appears to reflect larger structures within the culture, such as the relation of the individual to the social order" (in press:26).

One example of this phenomenon could be seen in the assignment of Mr. Knopf, a man in his eighties who had been diagnosed as hypertensive and disoriented, to a room on E section. When Mr. Knopf was first discussed by Mrs. Richter, the administrator, and her staff, he was described as "a nice, quiet man who is well placed." Such labeling contrasted with the more common descriptions applied to E patients, which emphasized the patients' alertness and the importance of immediately integrating them into ward social life. The brief reference in the staff meeting to Knopf as "quiet" and "nice," despite his acknowledged senility, was interpreted by the staff as an indication that (1) he was not to be included in E social activities and contacts, and (2) he would be allowed to remain an E resident as long as he behaved quietly and, so as not to upset others on the ward, as long as he was confined to his room. Mrs. Richter's words were later echoed by the nurse in charge of Mr. Knopf's case, who, in an interview with me, stated, "He stays pretty much in his room all day. This way he doesn't disturb anyone, but he is quiet. We don't bring him out to sit with the others much."

In other words, the original definition of E, as it was construed by staff and patients to be in contrast with the other wards, was maintained even with the Knopf assignment. Furthermore, the appropriateness and utility of such a differential ward structuring were upheld or, at least, went unquestioned in this case; the need to segregate the potential ward violator/disruptor from the others was expressed, and particular actions were initiated in this regard.

Sisters of Faith Home

Sisters of Faith Home (SFH) organized its system of assignments and reassignments on a different basis. The history of SFH's founding, and, perhaps more important, the administrator's selective reports regarding this history, indicated an institution-wide perception of nursing homes in general, and this nursing home in particular, as a charity and health-care facility for the aged. This emphasis is reflected in Sr. Marie's talk about the founding clergyman and the reputation that the Sisters of Faith brought to the facility when it was founded over seventy years ago:

Sr. Marie: I see a man way ahead of his time. We talked [sic] about it in [terms of] extended care today. But he was provid[ing] for that back then. . . .

And then they went to the bishop, who asked, well, he gave a list of names of communities to Father Welch but recommended Sisters of Faith. . . . And this was in nineteen I believe sixteen. We were already in our Home for Childhood Diseases in Boston. . . . And our reputation [for health care] preceded us.

SFH did not define itself simply as a domiciliary facility, but rather emphasized its role as a total-care medical institution.

Consonant with this definition of the institution as a whole was an assumption held by the staff members concerning their role vis-à-vis patients. The staff members displayed what might be interpreted as an all-encompassing helping attitude toward their charges. This differed from the impression the PH personnel seemed to present in their interviews with me and with applicant families. Staff members at People's Home asserted that their purpose was to assist the patients in helping themselves and to provide them with a fitting residential setting, not to "serve" them. In contrast, when SFH staff members were asked to talk about their nursing home, they referred first and foremost to the numerous health programs made available to patients, which extended beyond those required by state and federal regulations for skilled-care licensure. Those expanded services which were proudly talked about included high staff-patient ratios throughout the home and extensive social services and religious offerings. From the residents' perspective, it is noteworthy that when asked to describe life in the facility, they often called the home a hospital and tended to attribute more importance to the medical services provided by the staff than to the potential for peer interaction.

A second difference between People's Home and Sisters of Faith Home was that the latter was not based upon a ward system. SFH consisted of six residential floors in three connecting buildings: four floors in the two halves of the Main Building, which were built at different times, plus two floors in the Auxiliary Building, which was the newest construction (see figure 4–2). With the possible exception of the third floor of the Main Building, none of the six floors was explicitly allocated for a single patient type.[7] The admissions board and the social work department assigned a room to entering patients without apparent regard for the patients' medical and/or psychological diagnoses. Although an attempt was made to apportion staff workloads evenly throughout the facility by a relatively equal distribution of types of patients, the rules regulating initial admission/assignment decisions specified that any patient or patient type could be given any bedroom.

Since the outset of the chief administrator's tenure at SFH, guidelines had been established which encouraged the mixing of "confused" and "alert" patients throughout the facility. It is perhaps more accurate in this respect to say that SFH residents were placed in rooms rather than on floors. The unit of concern for this institution and its members was clearly the room or bed, not

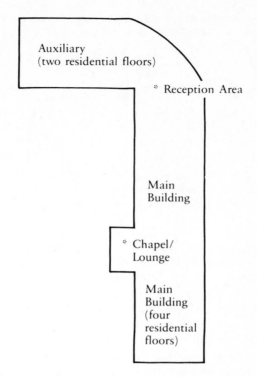

Auxiliary
(two residential floors)

* Reception Area

Main
Building

* Chapel/
Lounge

Main
Building
(four
residential
floors)

Not drawn to scale.

Figure 4–2. Layout of Sisters of Faith Home

the floor or section (which ostensibly had no defining features). In her interviews with me, the administrator expressed her aversion to the implications of a ward system, which conjured up images of locked wards in her mind, and a preference for continuing a general policy of integration that was said to have been established many years before by her predecessors.

These assignment/reassignment procedures were further justified and explained by the administrator and other key personnel on the basis of a conviction that SFH should provide the greatest possible service to the surrounding community. SFH described itself as obliged to admit all individuals who qualified for placement; it therefore made use of a waiting list that guaranteed applicants and their families an eventual placement in the facility. The absence of differential ward criteria was thus justified on the grounds that it increased the number of possible entry slots for applicants and hastened admissions. Social workers at Sisters of Faith Home were discouraged from leaving beds unfilled for more than a few days; this was considered to be a disservice to the community as well as economically unsound.[8] Finally, as suggested above, staff members claimed that patients must be treated as individuals. A ward system, from the SFH perspective, served to label and to group patients together, and this was to be avoided.

(Discussion with Sr. Marie during lunch): I ask Sr. Marie how it came about that residents (both confused and nonconfused) are scattered throughout SFH. . . . She tells me that it was her idea to mix the resident populations that way; she feels it's better for the confused. She says that the third floor used to be a locked ward before she got here, but "I have a problem dealing with restrained residents, with locking them in, probably because I wouldn't like it for myself." She says that she has no aversion to putting confused patients on the first floor, that she does not want to turn the first floor into a showplace: "I don't want to give families the wrong ideas. I'd put confuseds throughout the building."

The equivalence patterning of the residential sections shaped criteria and procedures for reassignments. Quantitative data indicated that transfers at SFH were as likely to involve intraward changes as they were interward changes (see table 4–2). The social workers and section nurses, who were in charge of monitoring the residents' behavior and deciding on reassignments, said that transferring off a section was not a necessary factor when deciding on a move. Consistent with the emphasis placed by the staff members on treating patients as individuals, personality conflicts between patients were cited as reason enough to justify a transfer, although these often involved intraward moves.

Table 4–2
Sisters of Faith Home Transfers

To:	From:					
	1M	*2M*	*3M*	*4M*	*2Aux*	*3Aux*
1M	1	5	2	3	0	0
2M	2	5	0	1	0	0
3M	1	0	5	0	0	0
4M	1	1	0	6	0	0
2Aux	1	0	0	0	2	0
3Aux	0	0	0	1	0	3

Source: These data are based on archival and/or observational records for January 1, 1980, to May 31, 1981.
Same ward transfers = 22 (55% of total transfers)
Different ward transfers = 18 (45%)
Same-type transfers (transfers between any two sections not involving 3M) = 15 (37%)
Different-type transfers (transfers between 3M and another section) = 3 (8%)
All equivalence transfers (same ward plus same-type transfers) = 37 (92%)

Transfers *off* a ward were often justified to remove a patient from a particular charge nurse's floor (by claiming the person was a "difficult personality"). Some of these patients eventually made the rounds of all the floors and charge nurses.

The concept of "personality clashes"—among patients, as well as between patients and staff members—was rhetorically consistent with the rest of the SFH typification vocabulary (cf. Schutz and Luckmann, 1973) for describing patients. Each transfer decision and associated account served to invoke the whole multilevel system of meanings regarding what it signified to be a patient in the institution, the structure of staff-patient interaction and obligations, and so on. The SFH rhetoric seemed to emphasize individual differences over section matching when explaining transfer decisions. In specific, differences and difficulties between patients were attributed to supposed individual characteristics of the patients rather than to inabilities to match or adhere to section-wide, supraindividual behavioral expectations.

A second situation associated with transfer decisions at SFH involved the changing health status of patients. When an individual was no longer deemed able to benefit from an existing slotting and from contact with his/her then current roommates, a room change might be initiated. Reassignments under these conditions were not necessarily intended to match the patient's deteriorating health status to the status of the room or floor—as was the case at PH. Instead, staff members described the proposed transfer location as a context that could stimulate and reactivate the regressed individual. This explanation seemed to echo the health-care mission held by the SFH staff members.

In some cases, "failing" patients were described by the staff as suffering from, and being particularly vulnerable to, the character of a then current slotting, which was itself subject to change over time. One problem acknowledged by SFH staff members was that without the benefit of a system that repeatedly assigned the same patient types to the same residential floors, there was little consistency in rooms over a period of time. Although the individual was not matched to ongoing criteria of a particular section or room, that is, to criteria that superseded specific persons then occupying places, there was some minimal attempt to bring specific residents together. An "oriented room" was not one that had been set aside exclusively for alert patients, but one in which the then current occupants were considered alert and personally compatible. These individuals might die, "fail," or be discharged, and the next round of occupants might be confused. While rooms at any point in time might be described by the staff using a particular label, over time these descriptions changed. It was not uncommon for patients to be given placements which the social workers initially assumed were appropriate but which eventually resulted in transfers. Staff members acknowledged that it was difficult to keep a room constant for other than brief periods, although no efforts at maintaining consistent room assignments were talked about or initiated.

Another implication of the absence of a ward system at SFH could be seen in the rules that guided interaction between residents and staff members, and among the residents. Room assignment was not as salient for the behavioral treatment of and expectations for patients as were "active"/"nonactive" labels. For the most part, different codes of behavior were not expected of patients with contrasting assignments, or of patients who experienced transfers. The use of physical restraints, tacit permission for patients to wander, and seating arrangements and locations, among other partials, were viewed by staff members as patterned for particular individuals, not for specific sections. Physical items such as wheelchairs and restraints were semiotically encoded, part of a code for meaning in the facility. Interestingly, at People's Home, the residents were aware of the meaning of bodily restraints, associating them with specific sections of the facility (A and C/D) and staff judgments of residents' behavior. Such was not the case at SFH: although staff members there indicated reasons similar to those at PH for restraining individuals, there was no indication that these reasons were in any way patterned with regard to the various sections.

Both residents and staff members distinguished those patients who were invited and expected to attend the homewide activities program from those discouraged from doing so. Nursing and activities personnel maintained that the former, the activities participants, were the alert members of the resident population and that the latter, the nonactives, were either senile or failing. Both patients and staff accorded the most prestige to those who engaged in the various programs in the activities room (see below for further discussion of differential notions of prestige). In part, such participation was considered an opportunity for extended sociable contact with peers within a constructive and productive work context, and for making a contribution to the church. With regard to staff-patient relationships, active residents tended to engage in more non–task-related interactions with staff members than did the nonactive residents. Active residents were provided with more situations (for example, afternoon snacks in the cafeteria, and so on) for sociable conversation with the staff. In addition, the flow of information concerning activities, events, and religious programs tended to favor the active patients over the others. Of course, the issue was not a quantitative one, but rather a question of the boundary conditions and access rules for focused talk. Specifically, only certain residents had access (in both a physical and social sense) to locations where non–health-related talk was likely, indeed expected, to transpire.

Thus, although the rhetoric of the administration at SFH might be seen as an attempt to deny or depreciate the existence of patient groupings and classifications, this institution did evidence practices that served to categorize and separate patients. SFH clearly drew a distinction between active/alert patients on the one hand and nonactive/senile patients on the other. This organization of patients was powerful, despite an emphasis on "individuality" as far as initial slotting decisions were concerned. Moreover, such distinctions as were drawn at SFH were coordinated with contrasting behavioral treatment by residents and by the staff. Such differentiating behavior was similar to that observed at PH. Differences in the behavior accorded patients based on their category were seen in terms of the physical spaces they were allocated for occupancy, their social relations with staff members, and so on.

Contrastive Observations

One influence on, or adjunct to, the differences in assignment criteria and procedures between the two nursing homes could be found in the contrasting goals and assumptions held by each institution. Although People's Home and Sisters of Faith Home were both confronted by a similar need to establish recruitment systems, the specific systems for assigning and reassigning patients to available beds developed in contrasting fashion. The recruitment systems differed in a manner consistent with certain other distinctions that can be formulated about the two facilities. The particular system each nursing home instituted seemed to be associated with its assumptions regarding the role of a geriatric facility in the care of elderly patients. Thus, the recruitment systems were apparently patterned not only by the social order requirement of functional continuity but by particular—and contrasting—institutional definitions concerning the place of health providers and skilled-care facilities in geriatric medical practice.

At People's Home there existed contrasting criteria for entry onto and position maintenance within each residential section. This range of criteria was ostensibly created to enable the institution as a whole to attract a variety of patients. It is interesting to note that SFH also seemed able to attract a diversity of clients, yet this occurred without the benefit or desire of a ward system. The differences in admissions and assignment procedures between SFH and PH seemed to be the behavioral outcome or concomitant of *the contrasting role(s) each institution defined for itself* and invoked when asked to explain general assignment/reassignment procedures as well as specific assignment/ reassignment decisions. Within the legalistic constraints of its skilled licensure (see Pennsylvania Department of Health, 1975), People's Home established its role as custodial and as the provision of a residential setting for aged individuals. This institution was defined in "social" terms, and a resident's ability to "make it"—that is, socially survive and adjust—in the facility presumed acceptance by one of the ward-specific patient groups, one of the ostensible attractions of the nursing home in the first place. In this manner, not only was there the requirement placed on PH of recruitment to fill available slots, but there was additionally the requirement of *differential recruitment* so that the institution could maintain the segregation of its relatively heterogeneous population.

In a sense, each slotting decision made by the administrator and each transfer decision made by the Health Care Review Team held a number of meaningful implications beyond the physical placement. Each slotting and transfer decision was multifunctional, invoking the repertoire of residential assignment discriminations as well as entailing definitions of social identity, careers, relationships, and so on within the institution.

As noted, SFH did not justify or explain the nonpresence of a ward system by its ability to attract applicants and patients, an ability evidenced by the long waiting list. Rather, certain other aspects of its self-defined responsibilities were important elements taken into account by the staff. SFH was defined by its administration first and foremost as a health-care center, one with a tradition of charity-related health services in the community. The administrative and nursing-staff members perceived their job as primary caretaker of the patients. Indeed, the patients spent several hours each day in servicing interactions with staff, and there appeared to be little emphasis placed on the establishment of contexts for resident socializing. The one situation in which a relatively small number of patients defined as actives did have an opportunity for peer interaction was arranged by the institution as a place for productivity. On the whole, it was the fulfillment of a Christian mission to provide aid to the sick and needy that defined Sisters of Faith Home.

The administrator of Sisters of Faith Home pointed out to me that there were two "schools of thought" that needed to be addressed when considering the relative merits of a ward system. Referring to the geriatric literature, the administrator noted that the data on the relative benefits of integrating versus segregating patients were ambiguous and inconclusive. A review of the literature supports this assessment (see Natenshon, 1969; Brody, 1970; Kahana, 1971). In a sense, then, SFH was faced with a choice between at least two approaches to the organization of geriatric facilities. The selection opted for by the administration was explained in a manner so as to be consistent with a "Christian" orientation: no segregation. As noted above, the administrator had an aversion to the implications of a ward system and a preference for carrying on a general policy of integration throughout the facility.

Each slotting and transfer decision at SFH was constructed in such a manner as to provide a residential placement, as well as to form and be part of a continuous set of messages that could be used to convey to outsiders, and to reinforce for insiders, the meanings that organized this facility. In contrast to PH, SFH was ostensibly constituted by equivalences among wards, among patients (and patient types), and among most interaction settings.[9]

It is not being suggested here that what can be called ideological differences between PH and SFH inevitably caused or resulted in the two contrasting recruitment systems. Rather, the present discussion attempts to demonstrate how the recruitment differences can be situated within a framework concerned with each institution's avowed goals and preferred tasks (see Sigman [1982] for a description of differences between the two institutions—for example, facility size—not pertinent to the present discussion). We are dealing here not with causality, but with the nature of the meaning structures patterning recruitment and the physical space.

These meaning structures can be related to the role of myth and ideology in social life. Campbell (1968) posits four functions of myth: (1) to provide cultural members with a common world view; (2) to legitimate existing institutions; (3) to locate the individual within the larger social order; and (4) to serve as a reminder of the mystery surrounding the other three. Relatedly, Deetz and Kersten (1983) provide four functions of ideology: (1) to support, stabilize, and legitimize existing order; (2) to exclude or interpret apparent contradictions; (3) to mystify existing order; and (4) to create consensus by controlling thought and action. Giddens suggests that what society members understand to be their social world comes to exert a powerful influence on that world: "Actors' own theories of the social systems which they help to constitute and reconstitute in their activities may reify those systems. The reification of social relations, or the discursive 'naturalization' of the historically contingent circumstances and products of human action, is one of the main dimensions of ideology in social life" (1984:25–26).

Thus, specific recruitment decisions invoked and entailed the mythologies and ideologies, that is, the avowed goals, tasks, and missions, as defined by each community. The differing attitudes regarding the degree and kind of health services found in each institution could be observed in transfer procedures. As noted above, certain transfers at Sisters of Faith Home were provided for failing residents and were intended to offer them a new and vibrant living context. These transition decisions reaffirmed and invoked the self-perception of SFH as a skilled nursing facility. In contrast, transfers of residents at People's Home were most likely to involve movement to a lesser ward, that is, one that the resident already "fit" rather than had to "live up to." These transfer decisions invoked and reaffirmed the priority of the differential ward system and the importance of patient-to-section matching.

As suggested above, one interpretation of these differences relates to the definition of its history, role, and responsibility to patients that each nursing home held. SFH viewed itself as a Christian health-care institution, caring for, and, in some cases, rehabilitating patients. While PH was also a skilled-care facility, it additionally viewed itself as a residential facility comprising varying living contexts. In this manner, reassignments at SFH were made in order to provide ameliorative living arrangements; at PH, in contrast, transfers were initiated with an eye toward furnishing a socially appropriate and minimally stressful environment.

The two institutions similarly differed with regard to their definitions of patient adjustments. When staff members at SFH talked about the adjustment of a new patient, they usually pointed to the patient's stabilizing medical condition, his/her enrollment in speech and physical therapy, and so on. On the other hand, PH staff members alluded to and stressed two other criteria when defining and evaluating patient adjustment: (1) the newcomer's becoming accustomed to navigating through the physical plant of the facility, and (2) the newcomer's acceptance into one of the ward-specific cliques.

Interestingly, patient-patient and staff-patient interactions at both PH and SFH remained largely consistent with the respective institutional (administrative) differences. Chapter 1 maintains that communicational predictability is a sine qua non for the adaptability and continuity of a social system. All social groups attempt to standardize and regulate the behavior of members: provisions are made for persons to have access to and command over some range of behaviors so that they can be considered predictable, and special treatment is accorded individuals whose behavior is insufficiently predictable to others. The behavior guidelines imposed on an incoming patient's conduct and the behavior accorded the individual by his/her peers and caretakers can be seen from this predictability perspective. Moreover, the various behaviors can be seen as part of what the decisions made by the admissions/transfer committees invoked when particular residential placements were selected.

Newly admitted patients interacted with their peers and with the professional staff in such a way that the subtle rules that constituted life in the facility became available to them. Staff members contributed to the patient's biography after the initial assignment in an apparent effort to ease the patient's "audition" vis-à-vis the other residents and to ease the patient's acceptance of the assigned position. For example, when Mrs. Ford was first assigned a room on E section of People's Home, no restraints were used by the staff to control her wandering. Although this effort failed and Mrs. Ford was eventually transferred to a different section, the initial attempt on the nurses' part was to facilitate Mrs. Ford's entry into and acceptance by the female clique on E. Similarly, the director of activities at SFH remarked that the first tasks given to new residents invited to join the activities program were simple ones; this ostensibly eased the adoption of the active label by providing the individuals with an initial success (especially since the newcomer was in full view of the veteran patients).

Monitoring interactions and patient labels also imposed standards of behavior on newcomers which they might (or might not) have attempted and been able to meet. In their interactions with their peers and with the professional staff, recent entrants to each nursing home were informed—explicitly and implicitly—how to conduct themselves with varic is others in the facility. Residents were informed about acceptable/unacceptable standards for behavior, as well as the consequences of not adhering to these standards. At PH, residents learned where they were expected to congregate and the conversational rules that governed interaction. Moreover, they learned what it meant to be an E, for example, and not a B or an A, and thus they became familiar with the classificatory scheme guiding social relations at the facility. The phenomenon of residents training each other was also evident at SFH, where many residents, even on the very day of admission, came to realize the importance of the labels "active" and "nonactive," and, in some cases, strove for a particular label to be designated for them. Information about these labels and their significance for social life at SFH was conveyed to recent entrants by the social workers during the admissions interview and by the residents' "welcome wagon."

Residents were able to find predictability in others (or assign this) through their efforts at continuous monitoring of each other's performances, by labeling the behavior they observed, and by sharing such information with a limited group of others (see Sigman, 1986). The novitiate's own behavior initiatives and reactions to the interaction he/she had with others were used by peers and staff members alike in an assessment procedure. The new resident provided information to others which was used to determine the appropriateness of that person for incumbency of the assigned social position; in part, this information was compared with standardized expectations (entrance requirements) sustaining a particular group's boundaries.

These surveillance procedures enabled veterans of the facility to find a category or classification for the behavior initiatives of others and to use this category in making determinations on the appropriateness, likelihood, and desirability of particular kinds of interaction contact with the newcomer.

As noted, one aspect of these frameworks of predictability at both facilities was that they were used by all members as guides for determining with whom one could "safely" have focused interaction, whose initiations of social contact were to be discounted, and the range of acceptable behavior (for example, conversational topics) when there was interaction. There was a regionalization of persons and encounters, such that there was "the 'enclosure' from view of some types of activities and some types of people and the 'disclosure' of others" (Giddens, 1984:xxv–xxvi). The behavior of the residents of both SFH and PH was guided by such procedures even though, as discussed above, differences in the specific behavior existed when the two institutions were compared. At PH, one's ward affiliation largely constrained whom one met on a regular face-to-face basis, and with whom one was expected to develop friendships. The expectations held about a new entrant were shaped by general background knowledge held about the particular section of assignment. The act of position assignment at PH could be interpreted to include the placing of a set of expectations that differed for each of the assignment types. After a period of time, during which staff members tried to provide for the patient's adjustment to life on the particular section and other patients conveyed the appropriate behavior rules, the insufficiently predictable individual was considered unsuitable for the particular section assignment and was moved. Insufficiently predictable persons were those who were unable to, or simply did not, meet the entailed behavioral obligations of the ward slotting.

The procedure operated differently at SFH. The initial framework of predictability was shaped not by the first position assignment, but by the subsequent invitation to the activities program. That is, particular courses of action large-ly ensued from the categorization of patients as either active or nonactive, not from a position in a residential section. Active residents avoided extended co-present interaction with those defined as nonactive and frequently disparaged staff efforts to include the latter in both recreational and entertainment activi-ties. Nonactive residents tended to remain on the floors for most of the day, usually sitting by themselves in the sun room or in a corner of their bedroom. In many cases, they appeared not to understand the system of values and iden-tity entailments at the facility (or, perhaps, they understood it all too well):

> *(Observation in fourth-floor lounge, SFH):*
> *Mae Olney:* It's quiet here today. The men, they speak all the time. It's usually all noisy. Y'know, they're crazy. I like it this way. Y'can listen to the TV. [*pause*] I wish they'd move that lady [in the wheelchair]. She's in my vision.
> *SJS:* Do you want me to do it?
> *Mae:* Would you? You better not, I don't want you getting trouble. [*to Catherine McGeorge:*] I told you what I told the nurse, nurse's aide. I said, "What do you feed them, crazy pills?" There's one man here, his wife's dead three years, an' he thinks I'm his wife. He wants me to come into his room. I don't do it. He calls me Myrtle. [*laughs*]
> *Catherine:* [*to me:*] The men all here are senile. [*to Mae:*] So we're here on the floor with all senile. They put us with a bunch of senile. They don't have 'em on the second floor. They got carpeting.
> *Mae:* You pay more money down there. I'd pay it. Well, you're senile and I'm senile. Well, I'm not senile. I'd be better off if I was.
> *Catherine:* Well, they c'n think it, but we're not.

Those residents who were not invited to join homewide activities during the day could be observed questioning their residential placement, and hence their sanity, apparently as a consequence of the patients they did come in contact with. This questioning often led to a doubting of one's own abilities and a bitterness toward staff members, since it was assumed that the latter consid-ered the resident to be senile. In this regard, one element consistently absent from staff discussions with residents and with visiting family members—especially during the initial admissions interviews—was information on the reasons for particular room assignments. Residents were thus left to their own musings and observations.

Patient categorizations invoked and entailed standards for the behavior of newcomers and also for the behavior of those doing the classifying—that is, social order categorizations had implications for the interaction order. This was especially the case at PH when newly arrived patients did not fit the highly limited ward-specific classifications. When an individual did not or seemingly could not conform to the expectations of the other residents (even after the training described above), then the latter residents shared their observations with each other and were apparently obliged to act upon these in particular ways. For example, patients were observed agreeing upon and/or imposing labels that could then be used to justify particular treatment to those whose behavior was nonconforming. Individuals who, despite the slotting provided by the staff, did not meet the audition requirements for a particular assignment, were defined as "crazy" or, more simply, as "not belonging." These labels were shared by the residents and were used to explain various orders of avoidance behavior (for example, conversational exclusions, activity cessations).

As noted above, both nursing homes evidenced prestigious in-groups that avoided contact with outsiders and whose boundaries were in part defined by their refusal to interact with other institutional actors. The existence of these groups and their relative status were, at least initially, organized at both institutions by the staff members; however, these groups were further sustained by interaction order rules adhered to by the residents themselves. Given the emphasis at SFH on entering a nursing home "for medical reasons" or "to be sick," it was perhaps not surprising that the women with the greatest status were those who transcended their illnesses in order to live relatively active lives. Further prestige was apparently allocated to those individuals who maintained or developed an attitude of contributing to church-related functions by accepting an invitation to join the daily activities program. In contrast, since People's Home was partially defined by the residents, their families, and the staff members as a place for establishing new friendships in one's later years, prestige was conferred on those residents who were not loners, who accepted the permanency of the institutional placement, and who eventually were included in one of the ward-specific cliques. Residents' participation in formalized activities was not considered by the staff members to be a salient characteristic of the "best" residents, although an individual's absence from his/her regular recreational events was occasionally interpreted as evidence of the individual's "failing" or "withdrawal."

The different labels or categories placed on patients were seen to be associated with a differential channeling of information from staff members to the patients. This was most clearly observed in access to knowledge about the various contexts of interaction, activity programs, and so on available at each facility. My observations indicated an interdependent relationship between particular patient position assignments and particular patterns of message flow. Residents who were assigned particular labels were made privy to certain information from and social relations with staff members. This differentially accumulated knowledge among the various resident factions served to maintain and reinforce the original distinct assignments. For example, SFH residents who were defined as actives were told about and invited to participate in various entertainment programs within the facility as well as in various excursions outside the home. Their participation in these programs served to provide the patients with information about additional social activities that were regularly scheduled by the nursing home and also extended contexts for non–task-related interaction with staff members and volunteers. The more a resident attended the various activity programs, and, moreover, the more a resident could be relied on by the staff to attend the activities they planned, the more likely was this person to be given future invitations. The staff members referred to the active residents' participation in social activities in order to justify the original assignments. The active residents, in turn, referred to their activities participation and their friendly relations with institutional personnel as part of a process that apparently served to disassociate them from other categories of residents.

At PH, message flow to patients was limited primarily by ward affiliation, although there also existed "open" contexts (for example, the beauty parlor) where homewide information was shared. Residents on each ward were told about only certain activities and about only certain physical locations of the total facility. Information boundaries were established through the residents' and staff members' talk as to where one might comfortably and appropriately enter. Nonassociation with institutional members outside of one's ward could be seen to reinforce one's belonging to the ward-specific group and one's seclusion from others at the facility.

Communication Streams and Invocation Reconsidered

This chapter considers the informational features of the various slotting and transfer decisions at People's Home and Sisters of Faith Home, and treats each environment as a patterned set of multiple messages, that is, as communication. For one, slotting and transfer decisions occurred through, and were accomplished by, communication interactions. Yet there is another, even more fundamental, sense in which the various slots and slottings can be seen to be communicationally appropriated and elaborated upon by both institutions. That is to suggest that residential placements—including assignment and reassignment activity, habitation of a particular ward or section, and so on—formed part of the system of message production constituting each facility. As noted, the definition of the individual message units (the slots or beds) and the total structuring of these units contrasted for the two facilities, constituting a set of beliefs about geriatric institutionalization and invoking meanings and rules of personhood.[10]

The slotting decisions at PH and SFH held different implications for the interaction, social, and semiotic orders; stated differently, slotting decisions partially contributed to, and were regulated by, each of the three orders of prime concern in this study in differential fashion. What is particularly interesting in the contrast between PH and SFH is the observation that the act of assigning a person to a bed in each facility can be seen to reverberate differently across the three orders constituting each institution.

What are some of the levels and orders that the data show were potentially available for invocation? Particular acts of assignment referenced several streams of behavior and regulative sets (codes) within the three orders: (1) the system of recruitment, or the need to remove "obsolete" slot fillers and to fill vacant slots; (2) the constraint of making selections and assignments—that is, of patients and wards—consistent with staff and family expectations; (3) the constraint of making selections and assignments consistent with an overall mission and ideology of each institution, or of giving the appearance of consistency; and (4) the entailed expectations and typifications for incoming patients' life courses, interactional contributions, and relationship reciprocals based on assignment and transfer decisions.

Although there was a certain predictable co-occurrence of units across these streams, that is, a particular assignment was designed to entail certain delimited messages consistent across the separate streams, this co-occurrence was to some degree limited in practice. The separate hierarchical streams were not co-terminus, coincidental, isomorphic overlays or transforms of each other. This was more readily seen at SFH, in which there was a great deal of "slippage" regarding the meaning of a particular bed assignment, that is, in terms of systems of meaning other than the purely recruitment one. And although the accountable ideology of PH professed a preference for there to be a clear, unequivocal, and unilateral meaning for each patient selection decision, there was "slippage" here as well. The administrative preference was for a particular slotting decision automatically to entail meanings within each of the separate code systems, that is, a particular slotting simultaneously was to reference and reinforce a message about the behavioral potential of patients, expected institutional biographies, and so on. In practice, however, a particular slotting decision represented a nonsingular articulation of the larger code and had to be further contextualized by the administration, nursing staff, and even patients. That is to say that via the mechanisms of the initial Health Care Review Team meetings and the audition interactions presided over by the residents, the "appropriate" hierarchical invocations were negotiated, developed, and projected (acted upon and used) by all institutional participants. The problematic nature of entailments could be seen in slotting decisions to B ward—which, as described above, developed an ambiguous reputation at People's Home—and in Mr. Knopf's "inappropriate" placement on E ward. Thus, when behavior was inconsistent or contradictory with expected entailments, the appearance of an ideology and the existence of a vocabulary of motives enabled one to act to some degree in relationship to potentially entailed and expected meanings (cf. Gerth and Mills, 1953; Stokes and Hewitt, 1976).

In brief, there were automatic entailments as partials of the codes for behaving—within an order and across orders—but there were also opportunities during performances for entailments to be negotiated, rearticulated, and recontextualized. Although this discussion has been about institutional life, I have also provided examples indicating the applicability of an invocations perspective to noninstitutional social life (cf. Goldschmidt, 1972; Pearce and Cronen, 1980; Rosen, 1984).

Summary

Social communication theory posits that the success or failure of communication cannot be judged by the criterion of isomorphic "sender" and "receiver" information states resulting from interaction. Indeed, success or failure is not necessarily a relevant criterion for the analysis of communication events in general. Differential access to behavioral codes—both in terms of production and interpretation activities—may give rise to communication events for which intersubjectively held rules and knowledge states are neither organizing features nor outcomes. In addition, the existence of a multiple invocation potential of behavior implies that social order messages—for example, ideological messages and messages about identity and relationship construction, inter alia—may go beyond what interactants "intend" to transmit.

Communication is the process of (society's) creating and sustaining meaningful differentiations of persons, objects, behaviors, and events. Social communication theorists recognize that such meaningful distinctions exist at a variety of levels within multiple orders; yet interacting persons are seldom aware of the polysemous nature of their conduct and can be seen to orient selectively to the multifunctional organization of their behavior. Instead of studying how individuals use rules to "create" messages, social communication theorists examine the underlying values associated with the rules of a particular society or group—that is, the social messages historically preexisting those which are intentionally and/or momentarily transmitted by the participants—as these both structure and are invoked (reproduced) by particular message "creations." Interpersonal moments involving "active" and copresent message design and production are partials that recreate and invoke the larger system of social messages and meanings. There are multiple orders, multiple codes within each order, multiple options within each code, and multilevel functions within each order, and interpersonal communication events are moments of such continuous social communication.

As evidenced in this chapter, decision-making processes, as one type of communication event, can best be studied not as a means of gaining objective information in order for persons to describe and control an external world, but rather as a means of invoking and using the information, categories, and guidelines that constitute a particular social world. Interactional moments involving and resulting in decision making can be analyzed from the perspective of the system of logics, the rules (Shimanoff, 1980; Sigman, 1980; Pearce and Cronen, 1981) which are followed and employed in arriving at and evaluating situations that require decisions to be made, and in arriving at and evaluating the decisions that are made. Smircich suggests that "within the boundaries of an organization there are multiple meaning systems, competing myths, and rival theories for understanding organizational experience" (1983:225). She indicates that this has implications for the way organizational members conceive of their responsibilities: "Strategic managers are not simply actors in their organization, rather they are the creators [and sustainers] of organizational symbols and realities" (1983:234). From this perspective, the nursing institutions described above are not simply contexts for administrative action and interpersonal communication; they are the continuous products of, and, in turn, the continuous constraints on, multichannel behavior.

The discussion concerning patient recruitment at People's Home and Sisters of Faith Home indicates that decisions made to admit, assign, and transfer residents within each facility occur in contexts structuring the range, meaning, and acceptability of decision options. The data show that multiple sets of socially generated values and procedures—in the present case, each institution's self-definition of its mission, the clients' attempts at entering prescribed interpersonal relationships, and so on—constrain and are reinforced by particular decisions. Each slotting decision, and each entailed and resulting patient career, must be seen (1) in light of the total set of possible meaningful distinctions established as part of each institution, and (2) as the momentary invocation and articulation of more encompassing codes of the interaction, social, and semiotic orders.

Notes

1. Although I am referring to *a* continuous stream, it is clear that this stream is hierarchically structured and composed of multiple subsidiary streams. The contribution that behavior makes to this total stream is thus multifunctional.

2. The absence of "choice" does not mean that behavior is without meaning. Giddens writes:

> But it is of the first importance to recognize that circumstances of social constraint in which individuals "have no choice" are not to be equated with the dissolution of action as such. To "have no choice" does not mean that action has been replaced by reaction (in the way in which a person blinks when a rapid movement is made near the eyes). (1984:15)

3. Observational and interview data were collected for five months in 1978 for People's Home and for nine months between 1980 and 1981 for People's Home and Sisters of Faith Home. As I reflect on it now, the choice of pseudonyms was (unconsciously) a value statement on my part regarding my experiencing of the two institutions: I am referring to People's Home as somehow "generic," or catering to people *in general,* while emphasizing the religious features of Sisters of Faith Home. These observations take on significance in light of the data collected and discussed regarding the recruitment patterns of each institution.

4. Different emic criteria produce either four or five distinct wards. As figure 4–1 indicates, a small section connecting A and E wards—labeled A/E—existed at the facility. A/E contained the nurse's station for it and for A section, but E-type residents were the ones assigned to its rooms. Although it would be possible to consider A/E a distinct ward, bringing the total to five, the administrative and nursing staff did not treat it in this manner. From the administrative point of view, A/E was reserved for the kinds of patients found on E and seemed to be considered an extension of that ward. In contrast, nurses assigned to the A/E station were responsible for both A and A/E patients and, in terms of feeding schedules, expectations for social activities, and so on, appeared to treat them similarly. In the present discussion, I consider A/E not to be a separate ward and, from the perspective of initial residential assignments, to be part of E.

5. There is a problem in the structuralist literature regarding how ambiguities similar to the B situation are to be handled. For example, Clarke writes:

> If an event A has the same permissible occasions of use as an event B, and B has the same occasions of use as C, then A shares all occasions of use with itself (the relation is reflexive), B shares all occasions of use with A (the relation is symmetric) and A shares all occasions of use with C (it is transitive). (1977:50)

Similarly, Pike indicates:

> In algebra, if a = b and b = c, then a = c. The [linguistics] student is likely to assume that if "x" and "y" are submembers of a phoneme, and if "y" and "z" are submembers of a phoneme, then "x" and "z" must be submembers of that same phoneme. This assumption holds true for data which are sufficiently detailed and accurate, but proves invalid for incomplete data. (1947:94)

The present analysis concerning B does not conform to these methodological strictures, apparently because of the diachronic (transitional) perspective used for data collection.

6. I am referring to "majority," but these quantitative data are significant only in light of the cultural themes that can be interpreted from the qualitative (observational and interview) data.

7. This ideal of a totally integrated facility was never realized during my fieldwork at SFH. The third floor of the Main Building had at one time been a locked psychiatric ward, and staff members and community visitors occasionally still referred to it in this way. As a result, the administration found it difficult to place alert patients on the floor.

8. See Sigman (1984) for an analysis of dialogue in which the staff members' understanding of these rules was gradually negotiated.

9. Missing from this analysis is a detailed study of the patients' relational reciprocals and the multiple implications of being a staff member of each facility. This is a limitation of the ethnographic data as collected (see Sigman [1982] for an elaboration of methodological choices in this regard).

10. Althusser writes:

> I shall then suggest that ideology "acts" or "functions" in such a way that it "recruits" subjects among the individuals (it recruits them all), or "transforms" the individuals into subjects (it transforms them all) by that very precise operation which I have called *interpellation* or hailing, and which can be imagined along the lines of the most commonplace everyday police (or other) hailing: "Hey, you there!" (1970:174; emphasis in original)

5
Summary

The Person in Social Communication

Social communication theory represents an attempt to build a theory of communication that is applicable to the full range of communication processes and situations—for example, "interpersonal," "organizational," and "mass"—typically isolated for study. It does this by suggesting that the analyst begin his/her research with a social group of whatever size in order to uncover the information-based activities the group continuously patterns and engages in. Taking the social group as the unit of analysis, social communication theory suggests that processes of group maintenance, adaptation, and/or integration are theoretically prior to processes of individual sensation or expression. This perspective does not deny the existence of either "subjective" experiences or biophysiological determinants of behavior; rather, it questions how these phenomena are appropriated, defined, and regulated by the particular social group under consideration. Expressional moments of interaction—that is, during which something presumed to be "inside" a person is "communicated to" another person—are seen as partial components of socially continuous behavior and as patterned by more inclusive social codes.

However, social communication theory is not built on a duality that separates the person from society, or the subjective from the objective. Rather, according to social communication theory, an individual member of society is also a *moment* in that society, a moment that has a recognizable (patterned) location in the group's process and structure. The social group is constituted by a differential allocation of resources for behaving in the form of code repertoires, and any single face-to-face interactional event in which persons engage is a moment in the continuous social communication process derived from these repertoires.[1] Similarly, subjectively experienced phenomena, for example, emotions and motivations, are constitutive of, and are regulated by, social repertoires; in specific, they represent partials of the behavioral codes reserved for *nonpublicly displayed social behavior*. In other words, so-called private experiences are segments of the continuous communication stream and are partials of the "objective" social world (cf. Carey, 1975).

Social communication theory is not concerned with the physiological and/ or genetic bases of individuals' experiences—although biological constraints and contributions are recognized as important—but rather with the social-meaning component of these experiences. Some biologically based differences, such as gender or hair color, may be communicationally elaborated upon by a particular social group. Other biologically based differences may not be communicationally patterned, a case in point being left- versus right-handedness, which today largely carries no contrastive meanings, although at one point in Western history it did (see the articles in Polhemus, 1978). But certainly not all or most of the categorizations and differentiations that are part of a group's communication system result from the "recognition" of biological differences. Thus, there are nonbiologically based, meaningful differences that are created and sustained by the social group. Religious and fraternity loyalties are two such differentiations. Finally, there is also a history of groups *creating* biological and physical differences which otherwise did not exist but which are meaningfully used as part of communication, for example, bodily alterations and adornments (Polhemus, 1978).

From this view, then, communication is the process of a group's creation and maintenance of meaningful differentiations between and among persons, objects, activities, and events. The rules or codes of communication are the structural parameters by which these discriminations are made and upheld, that is, constituted and regulated. The research agenda from the social communication perspective proceeds as follows: Instead of studying how individuals use rules to create their "own" messages, social communication examines the underlying values (messages) associated with the rule system and its social distribution. In this framework, those messages presumed to be intentionally and/or consciously transmitted from one person to another are seen to represent only a small portion of the total messagefulness of the communication "ecology."[2]

Communication is also the active process that differentially channels and locates messages or information within a social group, and, from the social communication perspective, is not the outcome or product of that process at any one moment. The latter qualification is important because it recognizes that communication organization is contingent upon inter alia the particular analytic "slice" from the temporal stream that is made, and upon the social identity of the "who" that is making this slice. As suggested in chapter 2, contrasting descriptive vocabularies can be used to account for communication regularities, and the choice of vocabulary relates to the "size" of the temporal context considered. Outcome-oriented models of communication tend to focus on the knowledge states of individual interactants and the degree to which these converge "before" and "after" interaction. Such analyses focusing on the immediate here-and-now of interaction fail to consider long-term functions and patternings of participants' similar (or dissimilar) information states and interaction rules.[3]

I emphasize the study of communication as process in order to avoid the more traditional approach, which views communication as a product or result, and, therefore, as something that can or cannot take place. Product-oriented views of communication can be spotted in two tendencies within the research literature: emphasis on "successful/unsuccessful" interaction, and on "input/output" variables. In the former case, communication is defined in terms of its outcomes, the assumption being that communication transpires, that is, "true" communication, when the message intentionally sent by one participant is completely received and understood by a second participant. The emphasis here is on isomorphic message production and reception by individuals. Communication in this dominant view is a commodity that can be more or less successful, and more or less turned on. In contrast, within social communication theory, communication is considered a continuous process that requires behavioral coordination, and not necessarily intersubjectivity, as participants adhere to supraindividual interaction programs.

In the second approach to communication as product, research emphasis is placed on those intraindividual (psychological), interpersonal, and situational variables which are presumed to influence message transmissions. These are seen to be prior to behavior, rather than part of continuous communication. In a sense, communication is itself "held constant" so that an analysis of the influences on it can be conducted. In contrast, communication within the social communication framework is considered a historical process, for the study of any one spatiotemporally bounded interactional event must be related to larger frames and contexts. These frames and contexts are not considered causes of behavior; rather, they are investigated as the more complex units that organize, and are constituted by, "smaller" units.[4] What occurs in any single interaction contributes to the continuities constitutive of this larger, through-time (historical) process.

As suggested above, the individual person is a moment in this social process; communication is the activity out of which persons are constructed. The person—in the sense of his/her identity, personality, disposition, and so on—is a moment-by-moment creation of communication.[5] This orientation can be clearly seen in the contrasting way interpersonal and social theories of communication conceive of participants' competence. Students of interpersonal communication seem to treat socialization as what society does to its members to prepare them for eventual competent behavioral productions; these competent performances make use of the socialization products (rules) as the individual goes about communicating to others. The social communication position is a different one. While it does not deny the requirement placed on society's members to learn appropriate behavioral repertoires, nevertheless social communication theory does not focus on the individual cognitive features of learning or on the representations of rule systems. Rather, it concentrates on what it means to continuously be a member of society, for example, on the differing partials contributed by relationship members throughout the life span to the identities of particular persons (cf. Goffman, 1959). Society and culture do not cause individual behavior; rather, they are constituted by the communication system which organizes meaning, that is, which enables behavior partials to be functional and significant. The socioculturally defined codes of which the communication stream is comprised serve continuously to construct and constitute persons as social actors or social identities.

From this perspective, there is no one time when an individual society member reaches some ultimate behavioral plateau (competence) from which communication is possible; rather, the individual is constantly engaged with others in the construction, affirmation, and reaffirmation of social identity and social competence. These constructions are vulnerable to various vicissitudes of social place and to the behavior partials contributed by others to his/her identity. In other words, part of the competence of an individual is contributed by relational and interactional reciprocals (see below).

Thus, the individual, even as he/she is being communicationally constructed, does not embody, or emerge with, the full spectrum of behavioral structures. As noted in chapter 1, there is a supraindividual patterning to be considered. Behavioral codes are not homogeneously or uniformly distributed in society, and they are not equally accessed by all society members. The individual may emerge (be constructed) as a moment of society, but it is important to emphasize that he/she is located as only a partial moment, contributing to and engaging in interactional activities and events only partially.

Signs and Symbols

One objection that might be raised against social communication theory is that the equation of information patterning with communication is too broad and inclusive for establishing a discipline and delimiting research areas. One recent proposal along these lines is advanced by Cronkhite (1986); a critique of this work below argues in favor of the present social communication position.

Cronkhite proposes that the rallying point of communication analysis is *human symbolic behavior,* with "symbol" defined in this case as a sign whose relationship to its referent is purely arbitrary (see also Peirce, 1958; de Saussure, 1966). Movement toward such a delimitation of the discipline is consistent in part with the present articulation of social communication because of its (1) social and (2) behavioral orientation. As a unit within a larger, conventionalized system of meaning, a symbol directs our attention to the society- or group-based organization of communication. Symbols are not in and of themselves meaningful or functional; rather, they take on meaning or function within a particular network of interdependent and interacting persons. The social group defines and regulates the appearance of symbols in interaction, and, in turn, is constituted and sustained by the organization of symbols. In this view, communication is (at least partly) activity involving the use of symbols, and is considered a preeminently social process: communication participants do not exist or behave in a vacuum, and their interactional events are inextricably bound to larger and more inclusive social contexts. Moreover, their behavior functions not only in (and for) the here-and-now of the interactional event but potentially contributes to a variety of more generalized, societally based activities (for example, recruitment, integration).

Although the present articulation of social communication encourages movement in the direction of symbolic activity as a focal point for communication study, I am nevertheless uncertain that such movement is adequately completed by resting with the symbol. My position here requires a bit of detailing. In his essay, Cronkhite (1986) suggests—and I largely agree—that the Watzlawick, Beavin, and Jackson (1967) assertion "One cannot not communicate" is a definitional statement and not an empirically verifiable observation about the world. Observations that seem to bear out the statement— that any and all behavior is seen to be communicative—are capable of doing so because the analyst collects and interprets data in such a way as to be consistent with the initial definition. While I agree with Cronkhite regarding the definitional status of the now classic maxim "One cannot not communicate," I disagree regarding its significance and its range of applicability to behavioral phenomena. Cronkhite suggests that while adhering to the proposition may be appropriate in the clinical setting (from which Watzlawick's work initially derives), it is not appropriate or "defensible" for a general definition of communication:

> To take that definition [that all behavior is interpretable and therefore communication] literally, especially outside . . . [the therapeutic] context, to try to elevate it to a *de facto* definition of the discipline, leads one to absurdity very rapidly. It is not that one *cannot* define "communication" so broadly as to include every behavior one can perform, including total catatonia. But it is hardly useful or advisable to do so. (1986:236; emphasis in original)

Cronkhite suggests, for example, that to consider perspiration or stomach grumbling—whether one's own or someone else's—as communication is an "awkward position" to be in.

Recognizing that my disagreement is in some senses "definitional" and that at some point disciplinary peers must agree to disagree on even fundamental definitions and then proceed with the task of research, I nevertheless am concerned by Cronkhite's delimitation. I also recognize that there is no corpus of data, no sensory experience of any kind, which can "validate" Cronkhite's or the social communication perspective (cf. Gergen, 1982). Nevertheless, I am uncomfortable with a totally relativist stance, and so argue strongly against the delimitation of communication solely in terms of the symbol.

There are a number of problems with excluding from the purview of communication analysis such nonsymbolic behavior as stomach grumbling and perspiration. To begin, the limitation to conventionalized (arbitrary) behavior is possible in the abstract only, not in actual practice. As a consequence of symbols being meaningfully rooted in particular group contexts, there is no universal set of behaviors, no pan-cultural repertoire of symbols, no a priori list of dictionary entries, which can be used to generate research. To know the symbolic status of a sensory event, that is, its semiotic status as a symbol, is for analysis to begin with the sensory event (etic behavior [Pike, 1967]) and then attempt to discover its role, if any, in a larger social repertoire (emic behavior). Such discovery can and does occur experimentally, ethnographically, interpretively, critically, and so on, but, no matter the methodology chosen, it cannot be known in advance by the researcher. The act of studying symbolic behavior does not begin with symbols, although it can lead to such understanding.

Given this consideration—that communication researchers must study behavior writ large in the process of uncovering, cataloguing, and interpreting symbols—social communication theory proposes that there may be reason to examine those behaviors which do not lead down the symbolic path, that is, ones which branch off along the larger semiotic road, as well as those which do. In other words, social communication suggests that the larger patterning of behavior into symbolic and nonsymbolic classes be addressed.

A number of potentially interesting research directions are opened here. One, for example, questions the importance of some behavior unit entering into symbolic coding for a group and another one not doing so. A second task questions the importance of a behavior unit entering into symbolic coding for one group but not for a second. A clear example of this is provided by Hymes (1974) in a reference to thunder. Within contemporary Western society, thunder does not "communicate to" people, although a set of interpretive rules exists which equates the appearance of thunder with the potential for a certain atmospheric event (rain). In contrast, some traditional Indian groups consider the appearance of thunder to be intentional "communication from" some entity (a deity) "to" them. In both cases, there is information or meaning generated, although, admittedly, one code hears the thunder as a "natural" phenomenon, as symptomatic of rain, and another as a manipulable "symbol." In either case, predictable (but noncausal) responses are generated by members operating within one or the other code. Social communication raises two questions about this situation: What can be said about a social group whose communicative contact is facilitated by atmospheric intermediaries? And what can be said about a group whose interpretations are "technical" and "scientific"?

This discussion leads to a second objection to Cronkhite's symbol proposal: A theory of communication must be culturally independent yet culturally sensitive. A theory of communication should be general enough so that no one group's approach to what constitutes communication is used as the sole basis for defining and delimiting the parameters of the discipline that studies it. In brief, such a theory must strive to avoid ethnocentrism. At the same time, it must be alive to the patterning of informative conduct in specific groups and to the nature of communication as envisioned by members of that group. This delimitation is inevitable, since, as noted above, symbols are socially rooted conventions. In this respect, it is interesting to ask how particular groups conceive of communication, that is, what is included in or excluded from acceptable communication (cf. Hymes, 1974; Katriel and Philipsen, 1981). Nevertheless, this does not mean that cultural definitions of communication can or should be used to derive a general definition. We must recognize that people behave and glean information in patterned ways that do not always adhere to explicit cultural definition. The sum total of means by which information is socioculturally patterned and experienced—whether the status of that behavior be assigned by the group (and analyst) to the category of natural sign or arbitrary symbol, and whether or not that behavior can be consciously attended to and explicitly labeled—forms the repertoire of behaviors appropriate to that group. If individuals as members of a code-using group make patterned interpretations and follow-ups to behavior, regardless of its semiotic status and degree of explicit cultural awareness, then it seems to me that the behavior is meaningful and a part of social communication.

As described in chapter 3, a distinction must be drawn between the semiotic origins of the behavior, that is, its recognition as informational within a particular group, and its interaction and social order appropriation (patterning) by the group. To limit analysis to symbolic behavior is to fail to see that people seem to behave simultaneously through multiple channels and unit types, and with regard to multiple orders. While the analytically discrete units of the multichannel stream have different semiotic statuses—they are variously defined and patterned to function as signals, signs, indexes, symbols, and so on—they can be seen to be patterned as an integrated whole when contributing to the total stream. The fact that one micro unit of behavior is a symptom, and the next a symbol—while of interest to the semiotician, who is interested in the nature of "signs" broadly conceived—fails to consider that they are organized in some fashion as part of the total social information repertoire.

Birdwhistell (1970) provides an example of a largely instrumental behavior (excessive toilet flushing) being meaningful within his family group (an indicator of wastefulness and moral weakness). Such behavior was not set aside by his family for purely symbolic communication purposes, yet the family members regulated their own moral standing and interpreted that of others with reference to this behavior. For cases such as this one, it is important that a theory of communication be sensitive to the variously patterned information sources employed within a network of interactants.

A more extended example can be used to show the multiple meaning structures at work in a community. Consider the case of a driver who notices a pothole in the road while driving his/her car. This pothole, which we will assume was not deliberately placed by a person, "provides" the driver with information for subsequently maneuvering the car.[6] The driver handles the wheel of his/her car so as to avoid the pothole. One might thus study individual drivers' reactions to the pothole, that is, the information value of the pothole for drivers. Differences in interpretation and reaction—there might, after all, be those who plow right in and do not avoid the hole—might be correlated with social demographic criteria of drivers, giving rise to an understanding of, for example, contrasting patterns of learning how to drive and contrasting conceptions of what it means to be a driver.

But the information value of the pothole need not be limited to the immediate driving situation. When various drivers return home, how does the "fact" that they encountered a pothole enter into subsequent discourse? Certain drivers complain about the conditions of roads to their family members, bitterly question how the ever-escalating taxes they pay are spent, and so on. These drivers call the local politicians whose campaigns they helped finance. Not only are they privy to these politicians' "direct" telephone lines, but the politicians immediately set into motion the necessary procedures for having the roads repaired. Other drivers do not know the appropriate means to reach their governmental representatives and experience no sense of power to influence the latter's actions; they bitterly and cynically believe that calling the politicians' general offices would be useless. What we eventually observe is that the roads the two driving groups cover look different and are constitutive of relatively distinct "neighborhoods."

From a social communication perspective, the message value of the potholes is greater than the terms established by driver avoidance reactions. Potholes become part of an information network distinguishing the environments that are inhabited by members of the, for example, upper and lower classes. It is important to note that these messages are not sent from one person to another; rather, they are part of the multichannel, multimessage, multiparticipant continuous stream that is social communication for the particular group. Of course, it is not the pothole as a product of physical environmental decay that is at issue here, but rather its social meaning appropriation.

In brief, social communication theory urges investigation of socially patterned and meaningful behavior, regardless of the semiotic status of any particular behavior or the group's explicit awareness and labeling of it.

Codes and the Social Communication Research Program

As can be seen, access to the continuous stream of communication—in the sense of knowledge about its organization and expectations for particular behavioral contributions—is restricted by persons' location in the social order. The analytic tools employed by social communication theorists to study social members' differential knowledge and contribution revolves around the following research goals:

1. Study the *code(s)* of logic by which the continuous production of behavior occurs with predictable regularity.
2. Consider actual *performances* of individuals making use of the code(s), that is, operating within and/or elaborating upon (articulating) the constraints.
3. Consider the *significance* of particular code structures available to individuals and groups, and of performance invocations and articulations, for the maintenance and/or change of the social order.
4. Analyze the *consequences for individuals* of the demands placed upon them by socially delimited communication rules, by the absence of such behavioral demands in certain contexts, and/or by the existence of contradictory ones.

The notion of "code(s)" is critical to social communication investigations. I select the term *code(s)* rather than *rules* for the locus of social communication analysis in order to emphasize the integration and interdependence of behavior units. A code consists of a set of related organizing principles (rules), which, in their integrated state, define the behavior of a particular communication modality or the constituent elements of a particular social scene or activity. A code can be thought of as a grammar that continuously regulates socially standard and acceptable behavioral performance through time, rather than as a rule specific to a single unit of behavior. A code can be *multichannel,* for example, a grammar for a particular event and the multiple units contributing to it (cf. Scheflen's [1968] definition of a "program"), or *monochannel,* for example, a grammar organizing a particular bodily information channel. In either case, emphasis is placed on multiple and integrated rules rather than on a single rule.

Codes can be analyzed with regard to one additional dimension, either as individual communicative *knowledge* or as aggregate social *pattern,* with the latter being the preferred mode for social communication research. That is, there can be, respectively, an individual- or a group-repertoire focus when writing codes. In the case of the former, social communication researchers study the numerous rules that particular individuals are expected to know and adhere to on the basis of their specific group memberships and socialization experiences. The emphasis here is on the partials expected of particular society members. In the case of the latter, social communication researchers analyze the multiparticipant behavioral demands that identity constructions, social activities, and contexts of interaction require for their complete performance (and, indeed, the very definitions constituting completion). As described with the notion of partials (see chapter 1), there is no assumption here that individual actors know or exhibit all the rules constitutive of the event or activity: rather, nonoverlapping, or nonisomorphic, rule sets are "joined" to form a supraindividual code. This supraindividual code represents a social repertoire that organizes and establishes individual repertoires.

Traditionally, the competence/performance distinction implies an inside/outside duality, in which competence is an individual's possession that exists prior to and independent of performance (cf. Chomsky, 1965, 1968; Hymes, 1974). According to social communication, descriptions of competence, in the sense of individual repertoire, are limited by the observational present available to the analyst, that is, the slice of performance actually studied. Further, competence is not separate from performance, and the latter is neither a bastardized nor a vitiated version of the former.

The behavior of the social system, and of individual society members, is continuous. Any moment of behavioral production, at the very moment of production, invokes both "competence" and "performance." Competence is not simply idealized knowledge that facilitates and thereby logically precedes performance. Rather, competence is the larger social-semiotic code (codes) which are called into play, which are invoked, at the moment behavior is performed. Competence is in a constant state of flux during performance in that the process of articulation serves to enable behavior to appear meaningfully and, at the same time, to "feed" itself back to the code structures (competence). Competence is continuously affirmed, reaffirmed, and/or altered by performance (performance articulations). In this respect, behavior can be studied in terms of its local sequential development—performance—and in terms of its encompassing hierarchies that are referenced and articulated—competence.

It should be noted that the notion of individual versus collective rules discussed above is not intended to mirror the inside/outside duality. The social communication approach suggests that all rules are socially generated and situated—they exist and are patterned by a group. While analyses may reveal an allocation of rules to particular individuals—a recognition that the division of labor is associated with a differential distribution of the code—social communication suggests that what the rules are "in" is moments of social structure, not people's heads. Competence does not exist inside the individual, for competence is conceived of as a relational proposition regarding social actors. Competence is a statement about the integration of behavior partials (the supraindividual code), rather than about the partials themselves. If an individual does not "know" something and is not held responsible for this knowledge, but is able to access it from another, as in the case of a family's collective memory (cf. Kaplan, 1981), then competence exists in (can be assigned by the analyst to) the interactional network and not necessarily the person.

This discussion returns us to the proposition that communication transpires with the participants holding nonisomorphic rules. If communication is considered to be a process that requires coordinated and intercalated performances by all participants, rather than a single outcome of behaving, then the existence of differential and multiple codes and meanings for behavior poses little theoretical problem. Indeed, the persistence of contrasting rules and interpretations, as these are related to the differential allocation of social-semiotic resources throughout a group and to status distinctions within the social order of that group, becomes a critical topic for social communication investigation (Hymes, 1974). The existence of code differences and information boundaries (reportability rules) implicates a more general, societally defined nonequivalence of the communication participants and their respective group memberships. In this manner, communication may ratify differences rather than produce similarities.

Notes

1. The term *face-to-face interaction,* although used throughout this book and by many authors, may ultimately prove to be misleading and ethnocentric. Data provided by Richards (1939) indicate that mealtime for the Bemba of Zambia (formerly Northern Rhodesia) is conducted with the participants orienting back-to-back and not face-to-face.

2. I am not suggesting here that the transmission model is a useful way to proceed (cf. Carey, 1975). In addition to the other problems discussed in this book, the transmission model confuses the organismic (physical) boundaries of the person—for which it is possible to say that messages are contained "inside"—with the social relational and interactional boundaries of the person (cf. Mead's [1934] concept of "mind").

3. Systematic differences in the description of communication patterning are also likely to be associated with the describers' "internality" or "externality" to the situation, for example, whether they are/were participants to, or observers of, the scene, and with the nature of their contribution, if any, to that scene.

4. A unit can be seen to have both *structure,* in the sense of an "internal" arrangement of its constituents, and *patterning,* or "external" relations with units of a comparable size.

5. From one perspective, *reconstruction* and *recreation* may be better words to describe this process, because they avoid the implication that the individual is produced anew each time during interaction (see chapter 1). Social communication emphasizes the historical givenness of person construction, for example, the existing places and allocations within the social order. However, one problem with *reconstruction* is that it implies a construction at one moment in time separated from a reconstruction at a later moment; thus it potentially fails to capture a sense of continuing process, which is key to social communication.

6. In a technical sense, objects do not provide or have information but rather are usable with regard to information value to someone. The information value of the pothole lies in the relationship between its appearance and the driver's (preceding and proceeding) behavior. Thus, by *information* I am not referring to an event that has some objective or independent status in the world. Rather, I am referring to conduct, in its broadest sense, which has a patterned location and is responded to as meaningful within some social group. An important aspect of information is its patterned distribution: it is situated in selected interactional events and for access by particular interactional participants.

Bibliography

Aberle, D.F., Cohen, A.K., Davis, A.K., Levy, M.J., Jr., and Sutton, F.X. (1950). "The Functional Prerequisites of a Society," *Ethics,* vol. 6, 100–111.

Albee, E. (1962). *Who's Afraid of Virginia Woolf?* New York: Atheneum Publishers.

Aldrich, H. (1972). "Sociability in Mensa: Characteristics of Interaction among Strangers," *Urban Life and Culture,* vol. 1, 167–186.

Althusser, L. (1970). *Lenin and Philosophy and Other Essays.* New York: Monthly Review Press.

Annandale, E. (1985). "Work Roles and Definitions of Patient Health," *Qualitative Sociology,* vol. 8, 124–148.

Aragon, L.V. (1978). "Topics of Conversation: A Study of Patterns in Social Discourse," unpublished M.A. thesis, University of Pennsylvania.

Archer, M.S. (1982). "Structuration versus Morphogenesis: On Combining Structure and Action," *British Journal of Sociology,* vol. 33, 455–483.

Austin, J.L. (1971). "Performative-Constative," in *The Philosophy of Language,* J.R. Searle (ed.). Oxford: Oxford University Press, pp. 13–22.

———. (1965). *How to Do Things with Words.* New York: Oxford University Press.

Axelrod, R. (1977). "Argumentation in Foreign Policy Settings," *Journal of Conflict Resolution,* vol. 21, 727–756.

Bateson, G. (1980). *Mind and Nature.* New York: Bantam.

———. (1972). *Steps to an Ecology of Mind.* New York: Ballantine Books.

———. (1953). "The Position of Humor in Human Communication," in *Cybernetics: Circular Causal and Feedback Mechanisms in Biological and Social Sciences, Transactions of the Ninth Conference,* H.V. Foerster (ed.). New York: Josiah Macy, Jr., Foundation.

Beach, W.A. (1983). "Background Understandings and the Situated Accomplishment of Conversational Telling-Expansions," in *Conversational Coherence,* R.T. Craig and K. Tracy (eds.). Beverly Hills, Calif.: Sage, pp. 196–221.

Becker, H.S. and Strauss, A.L. (1956). "Careers, Personality, and Adult Socialization," *American Journal of Sociology,* vol. 62, 253–263.

Berger, A.A. (1984). *Signs in Contemporary Culture: An Introduction to Semiotics.* New York: Longman.

Berger, P.L. (1963). *Invitation to Sociology: A Humanistic Perspective.* Garden City, N.Y.: Doubleday Anchor.

Berger, P.L. and Luckmann, T. (1967). *The Social Construction of Reality.* Garden City, N.Y.: Doubleday Anchor.

Bernstein, B. (1975). *Class, Codes and Control: Theoretical Studies Towards a Sociology of Language.* New York: Schocken.

Birdwhistell, R.L. (1977). "Some Discussion of Ethnography, Theory, and Method," in *About Bateson,* J. Brockman (ed.). New York: Dutton, pp. 103–141.

———. (1970). *Kinesics and Context.* Philadelphia: University of Pennsylvania Press.

———. (1952). *Introduction to Kinesics.* Washington, D.C.: Foreign Service Institute.

Bloomfield, L. (1933). *Language.* New York: Holt, Rinehart and Winston.

Blum, A.F. and McHugh, P. (1971). "The Social Ascription of Motives," *American Sociological Review,* vol. 36, 98–109.

Blumer, H. (1969). *Symbolic Interactionism.* Englewood Cliffs, N.J.: Prentice-Hall.

Bormann, E.G. (1983). "Symbolic Convergence: Organizational Communication and Culture," in *Communication and Organizations: An Interpretive Approach,* L.L. Putnam and M.E. Pacanowsky (eds.). Beverly Hills, Calif.: Sage, pp. 99–122.

Brody, E.M. (1970). "Congregate Care Facilities and Mental Health of the Elderly," *International Journal of Aging and Human Development,* vol. 1, 279–321.

Brown, R. and Ford, M. (1961). "Address in American English," *Journal of Abnormal and Social Psychology,* vol. 62, 375–385.

Butterworth, B. (1978). "Maxims for Studying Conversations," *Semiotica,* vol. 24, 317–339.

Buttny, R. (in press). "Sequence and Practical Reasoning in Accounts Episodes," *Communication Quarterly,* vol. 35.

———. (1985). "Accounts as a Reconfiguration of an Event's Context," *Communication Monographs,* vol. 52, 57–76.

Campbell, J. (1968). *Masks of God.* Vol. 4, *Creative Mythology.* New York: Viking.

Carey, J.W. (1975). "A Cultural Approach to Communication," *Communication,* vol. 2, 1–22.

Chomsky, N. (1968). *Language and Mind.* New York: Harcourt, Brace and World.

———. (1965). *Aspects of the Theory of Syntax.* Cambridge, Mass.: MIT Press.

Cicourel, A.V. (1980a). "Language and Social Interaction: Philosophical and Empirical Issues," *Sociological Inquiry,* vol. 50, 1–30.

———. (1980b). "Three Models of Discourse Analysis," *Discourse Processes,* vol. 3, 101–132.

Clark, H.H. and Haviland, S.E. (1977). "Comprehension and the Given-New Contract," in *Discourse Production and Comprehension,* R.O. Freedle (ed.). Norwood, N.J.: Ablex, pp. 1–40.

Clarke, D.D. (1977). "Rules and Sequences in Conversation," in *Social Rules and Social Behaviour,* P. Collett (ed.). Oxford: Basil Blackwell, pp. 42–69.

Collins, R. (1985). *Three Sociological Traditions.* New York: Oxford University Press.

Condon, W.C. (1980). "The Relation of Interactional Synchrony to Cognitive and Emotional Process," in *The Relationship of Verbal and Nonverbal Communication,* M.R. Key (ed.). The Hague: Mouton, pp. 49–65.

Corsaro, W.A. (1982). "Something Old and Something New: The Importance of Prior Ethnography in the Collection and Analysis of Audiovisual Data," *Sociological Methods and Research,* vol. 11, 145–166.

Coulter, J. (1985). "Two Concepts of the Mental," in *The Social Construction of the Person,* K.J. Gergen and K.E. Davis (eds.). New York: Springer-Verlag, pp. 167–189.

Coulthard, M. (1977). *An Introduction to Discourse Analysis.* London: Longman.

Craig, R.T. and Tracy, K. (eds.). (1983). *Conversational Coherence.* Beverly Hills, Calif.: Sage.

Crane, D. (1972). *Invisible Colleges: Diffusion of Knowledge in Scientific Communities.* Chicago: University of Chicago Press.

Cronen, V.E., Pearce, W.B., and Tomm, K. (1985). "A Dialectical View of Personal Change," in *The Social Construction of the Person,* K.J. Gergen and K.E. Davis (eds.). New York: Springer-Verlag, pp. 203–224.

Cronkhite, G. (1986). "On the Focus, Scope, and Coherence of the Study of Human Symbolic Activity," *Quarterly Journal of Speech,* vol. 72, 231–246.

Csikszentmihalyi, M. and Rochberg-Halton, E. (1981). *The Meaning of Things: Domestic Symbols and the Self.* Cambridge: Cambridge University Press.

Cushman, D.P. (1980). "A Functional Approach to Rules Research." Paper presented to the Eastern Communication Association, Ocean City, Maryland.

Deetz, S.A. and Kersten, A. (1983). "Critical Models of Interpretive Research," in *Communication and Organizations: An Interpretive Approach,* L.L. Putnam and M.E. Pacanowsky (eds.). Beverly Hills, Calif.: Sage, pp. 147–171.

Denzin, N.K. (1984). *On Understanding Emotion.* San Francisco: Jossey-Bass.

de Saussure, F. (1966). *Course in General Linguistics.* New York: McGraw-Hill.

Donohue, W.A., Cushman, D.P., and Nofsinger, R.E. (1980). "Creating and Confronting Social Order: A Comparison of Rules Perspectives," *Western Journal of Speech Communication,* vol. 44, 5–19.

Duncan, S., Jr. (1972). "Some Signals and Rules for Taking Speaking Turns in Conversations," *Journal of Personality and Social Psychology,* vol. 23, 283–292.

Durkheim, E. (1938). *The Rules of the Sociological Method.* Chicago: University of Chicago Press.

———. (1933). *The Division of Labor in Society.* New York: Free Press.

Erickson, F. and Shultz, J. (1982). *The Counselor as Gatekeeper: Social Interaction in Interviews.* New York: Academic Press.

———. (1981). "When Is a Context? Some Issues and Methods in the Analysis of Social Competence," in *Ethnography and Language in Educational Settings,* J. Green and C. Wallat (eds.). Norwood, N.J.: Ablex, pp. 147–160.

Ervin-Tripp, S. (1976). "Is Sybil There?: The Structure of Some American English Directives," *Language in Society,* vol. 5, 25–66.

———. (1972). "On Sociolinguistic Rules: Alternation and Co-occurrence," in *Directions in Sociolinguistics,* J.J. Gumperz and D. Hymes (eds.). New York: Holt, Rinehart and Winston, pp. 213–250.

Fisher, B.A. (1978). *Perspectives on Human Communication.* New York: Macmillan.

Fowler, R., Hodge, B., Kress, G., and Trew, T. (1979). *Language and Control.* London: Routledge & Kegan Paul.

Frentz, T.S. and Farrell, T.B. (1976). "Language-Action: A Paradigm for Communication," *Quarterly Journal of Speech,* vol. 62, 333–349.

Geertz, C. (1975). "On the Nature of Anthropological Understanding," *American Scientist,* vol. 63, 47–53.

Geertz, C. (1960). *The Religion of Java.* Glencoe, Ill.: Free Press.

Gergen, K.J. (1982). *Toward Transformation in Social Knowledge.* New York: Springer-Verlag.

Gergen, K.J. and Davis, K.E. (eds.). (1985). *The Social Construction of the Person.* New York: Springer-Verlag.

Gerth, H. and Mills, C.W. (1953). *Character and Social Structure.* New York: Harcourt, Brace and Co.

Giddens, A. (1984). *The Constitution of Society.* Berkeley: University of California Press.

Glaser, B.G. and Strauss, A.L. (1971). *Status Passage.* Chicago: Aldine-Atherton.

Goffman, E. (1983a). "The Interaction Order," *American Sociological Review,* vol. 48, 1–17.

———. (1983b). "Felicity's Condition," *American Journal of Sociology,* vol. 89, 1–53.

———. (1979). Class lecture, University of Pennsylvania.

———. (1974). *Frame Analysis.* New York: Harper and Row.

———. (1971). *Relations in Public.* New York: Harper and Row.

———. (1969). *Strategic Interaction.* Philadelphia: University of Pennsylvania Press.

———. (1967). *Interaction Ritual.* Chicago: Aldine.

———. (1963). *Behavior in Public Places.* New York: Free Press.

———. (1961a). *Asylums.* Garden City, N.Y.: Doubleday Anchor.

———. (1961b). *Encounters: Two Studies in the Sociology of Interaction.* Indianapolis: Bobbs-Merrill.

———. (1959). *The Presentation of Self in Everyday Life.* Garden City, N.Y.: Doubleday Anchor.

Goldberg, J.A. (1983). "A Move Toward Describing Conversational Coherence," in *Conversational Coherence,* R.T. Craig and K. Tracy (eds.). Beverly Hills, Calif.: Sage, pp. 25–45.

Golding, P. and Murdock, G. (1978). "Theories of Communication and Theories of Society," *Communication Research,* vol. 5, 339–356.

Goldschmidt, W. (1972). "An Ethnography of Encounters: A Methodology for the Enquiry into the Relation between the Individual and Society," *Current Anthropology,* vol. 13, 59–78.

Gouldner, A.W. (1970). *The Coming Crisis of Western Sociology.* New York: Basic Books.

Grice, H.P. (1975). "Logic and Conversation," in *Syntax and Semantics.* Vol. 3, *Speech Acts,* P. Cole and J.L. Morgan (eds.). New York: Academic Press, pp. 41–58.

Gumperz, J.J. (1982). *Discourse Strategies.* Cambridge: Cambridge University Press.

Hall, E.T. (1984). *The Dance of Life.* Garden City, N.Y.: Doubleday Anchor.

Halliday, M.A.K. (1978). *Language as Social Semiotic: The Social Interpretation of Language and Meaning.* London: Edward Arnold.

Handel, W. (1982). *Ethnomethodology: How People Make Sense.* Englewood Cliffs, N.J.: Prentice-Hall.

Harré, R. (1979). *Social Being.* Totowa, N.H.: Littlefield, Adams, and Co.

Harré, R., Clarke, D., and DeCarlo, N. (1985). *Motives and Mechanisms: An Introduction to the Psychology of Action.* London: Methuen.

Harris, Z. (1951). *Methods in Structural Linguistics.* Chicago: University of Chicago Press.

Harwood, A. (ed.). (1981). *Ethnicity and Medical Care.* Cambridge, Mass.: Harvard University Press.

Hawes, L.C. (1974). "Social Collectivities as Communication: Perspective on Organizational Behavior," *Quarterly Journal of Speech,* vol. 60, 497–502.

Heilman, S.C. (1979). "Communication and Interaction: A Parallel in the Theoretical Outlooks of Erving Goffman and Ray Birdwhistell," *Communication,* vol. 4, 221–234.

Heritage, J.C. and Watson, D.R. (1979). "Formulations as Conversational Objects," in *Everyday Language: Studies in Ethnomethodology,* G. Psathas (ed.). New York: Irvington, pp. 123–162.

Hochschild, A.R. (1983). *The Managed Heart.* Berkeley: University of California Press.

Hockett, C.F. (1958). *A Course in Modern Linguistics.* New York: Macmillan.

Hopper, R. (1983). "Interpretation as Coherence Production," in *Conversational Coherence,* R.T. Craig and K. Tracy (eds.). Beverly Hills, Calif.: Sage, pp. 81–98.

———. (1981). "The Taken-for-Granted," *Human Communication Research,* vol. 7, 195–211.

Hymes, D. (1974). *Foundations in Sociolinguistics.* Philadelphia: University of Pennsylvania Press.

Irvine, J.T. (1974). "Strategies of Status Manipulation in the Wolof Greeting," in *Explorations in the Ethnography of Speaking,* R. Bauman and J. Sherzer (eds.). New York: Cambridge University Press, pp. 167–191.

Jackson, S.A. (1983). "Speech Acts as the Basis for Conversational Coherence." Paper presented to the Speech Communication Association, Washington, D.C.

Jackson, S.A. and Jacobs, S. (1980). "Structure of Conversational Argument: Pragmatic Bases for the Enthymeme," *Quarterly Journal of Speech,* vol. 66, 251–265.

Jakobson, R. (1960). "Closing Statement: Linguistics and Poetics," in *Style in Language,* T. Sebeok (ed.). Cambridge, Mass.: MIT Press, pp. 350–377.

Joos, M. (1967). *The Five Clocks.* New York: Harcourt, Brace and World.

Kahana, E. (1971). "Emerging Issues in Institutional Services for the Aging," *Gerontologist,* vol. 11, 51–58.

Kaplan, H. (1981). "The Social Organization of Memory: An Inquiry into the Structural Arrangements and Communicative Processes Which Provide for Information Storage and Retrieval in Social Groups," unpublished M.A. thesis, University of Pennsylvania.

Katcher, A.H. and Beck, A.M. (eds.). (1983). *New Perspectives on Our Lives with Companion Animals.* Philadelphia: University of Pennsylvania Press.

Katriel, T. and Philipsen, G. (1981). " 'What We Need Is Communication': 'Communication' as a Cultural Category in Some American Speech," *Communication Monographs,* vol. 48, 301–317.

Keenan, E.O. (1973). "The Universality of Conversational Postulates," *Language in Society,* vol. 5, 67–80.

Keenan, E.O. and Schieffelin, B.B. (1976). "Topic as a Discourse Notion: A Study of Topic in the Conversations of Children and Adults," in *Subject and Topic,* C.N. Li (ed.). New York: Academic Press, pp. 335–384.

Kemper, T.D. (1972). "The Division of Labor: A Post-Durkheimian Analytical View," *American Sociological Review,* vol. 37, 739–753.

Kendon, A. (1982). "The Organization of Behavior in Face-to-Face Interaction: Observations on the Development of a Methodology," in *Handbook of Methods in Nonverbal Behavior Research,* K.R. Scherer and P. Ekman (eds.). Cambridge: Cambridge University Press, pp. 440–505.

———. (1977). *Studies in the Behavior of Social Interaction.* Bloomington, Ind.: Indiana University Press, and Lisse, The Netherlands: Peter de Ridder.

Kersten, A. (1986). "Critical Research and the Problem of Multi-Level Analysis: Notes on Connecting Micro Events and Macro Structures." Paper presented to the International Communication Association, Chicago.

Kockelmans, J.J. (1975). "Toward an Interpretative or Hermeneutic Social Science," *Graduate Faculty Philosophy Journal,* vol. 5, 73–96.

Kreckel, M. (1981). *Communicative Acts and Shared Knowledge in Natural Discourse.* London: Academic Press.

Kroeber, A.L. (1963). *Anthropology: Culture Patterns and Processes.* New York: Harcourt Brace Jovanovich.

LaBarre, W. (1954). *The Human Animal.* Chicago: University of Chicago Press.

Lasswell, H.D. (1971). "The Structure and Function of Communication in Society," in *The Process and Effects of Mass Communication,* W. Schramm and D.F. Roberts (eds.). Urbana, Ill.: University of Illinois Press, pp. 84–99.

Leach, E. (1976). *Culture and Communication.* Cambridge: Cambridge University Press.

Leeds-Hurwitz, W. (1986). "Erving Goffman and the Concept of Social Order." Paper presented to the Conference, Erving Goffman: An Interdisciplinary Appreciation, University of York, England.

Levinson, S.C. (1983). *Pragmatics.* Cambridge: Cambridge University Press.

Linton, R. (1942). "Age and Sex Categories," *American Sociological Review,* vol. 7, 589–603.

———. (1940). "A Neglected Aspect of Social Organization," *American Journal of Sociology,* vol. 45, 870–886.

———. (1936). *The Study of Man.* New York: Appleton-Century-Crofts.

Lundberg, G. (1939). *Foundations of Sociology.* New York: Macmillan.

MacCannell, D. (1983). "Commemorative Essay: Erving Goffman (1922–1982)," *Semiotica,* vol. 45, 1–33.

Malinowski, B. (1923). "The Problem of Meaning in Primitive Languages," supplement to *The Meaning of Meaning,* by C.K. Ogden and I.A. Richards. New York: Harcourt Brace Jovanovich, pp. 296–336.

Mandelbaum, M. (1973). "Societal Facts," in *Modes of Individualism and Collectivism,* J. O'Neill (ed.). London: Heinemann, pp. 221–234.

Markson, E. (1971). "A Hiding Place to Die," *Transaction,* vol. 9, 48–54.

Mathiot, M. (1983). "Toward a Meaning-Based Theory of Face-to-Face Interaction," *International Journal of the Sociology of Language,* vol. 43, 5–56.

McCall, G.J. and Simmons, J.L. (1978). *Identities and Interactions,* revised edition. New York: Free Press.

McLaughlin, M.L., Cody, M.J., and Rosenstein, N.E. (1983). "Account Sequences in Conversations between Strangers," *Communication Monographs,* vol. 50, 102–125.

McNeill, D. (1985). "So You Think Gestures Are Nonverbal?" *Psychological Review,* vol. 92, 350–371.

Mead, G.H. (1934). *Mind, Self, and Society.* Chicago: University of Chicago Press.

Merton, R.K. (1968). *Social Theory and Social Structure,* enlarged edition. New York: Free Press.

Natenshon, L.J. (1969). "The Architectural Dilemma: Design, Individual Needs, and Social Living," *Gerontologist,* vol. 9, 60–65.

Nofsinger, R.E. (1983). "Tactical Coherence in Courtroom Conversation," in *Conversational Coherence,* R.T. Craig and K. Tracy (eds.). Beverly Hills, Calif.: Sage, pp. 243–258.

———. (1977). "A Peek at Conversational Analysis," *Communication Quarterly,* vol. 25, 12–20.

———. (1975). "The Demand Ticket: A Conversational Device for Getting the Floor," *Speech Monographs,* vol. 42, 1–9.

Nwoye, G. (1985). "Eloquent Silence among the Igbo of Nigeria," in *Perspectives on Silence,* D. Tannen and M. Saville-Troike (eds.). Norwood, N.J.: Ablex, pp. 185–191.

O'Neill, J. (ed.). (1973). *Modes of Individualism and Collectivism.* London: Heinemann.

Pacanowsky, M.E. and O'Donnell-Trujillo, N. (1983). "Organizational Communication as Cultural Performance," *Communication Monographs,* vol. 50, 126–147.

Parker, R. (1984). "Conversational Grouping and Fragmentation: A Preliminary Investigation," *Semiotica,* vol. 50, 43–68.

Pearce, W.B. (1977). "Naturalistic Study of Communication: Its Function and Form," *Communication Quarterly,* vol. 25, 51–56.

Pearce, W.B. and Cronen, V.E. (1980). *Communication, Action, and Meaning: The Creation of Social Realities.* New York: Praeger.

Peirce, C.S. (1958). *The Collected Papers of C.S. Peirce,* vols. 1–6, C. Hartshorne and P. Weiss (eds.), 1931–35; vols. 7–8, A.W. Burks (ed.), 1958. Cambridge, Mass.: Harvard University Press.

Pennsylvania Department of Health. (1975). *Long-Term Care Facilities Licensure Regulations.*

Piaget, J. (1970). *Structuralism.* New York: Basic Books.

Pike, K.L. (1967). *Language in Relation to a Unified Theory of the Structure of Human Behavior.* The Hague: Mouton.

———. (1947). *Phonemics: A Technique for Reducing Languages to Writing.* Ann Arbor, Mich.: University of Michigan Press.

Pittenger, R.E., Hockett, C.F., and Danehy, J.J. (1960). *The First Five Minutes: A Sample of Microscopic Interview Analysis.* Ithaca, N.Y.: Paul Martineau.

Polhemus, T. (ed.). (1978). *The Body Reader: Social Aspects of the Human Body.* New York: Pantheon Books.

Poole, M.S. and McPhee, R.D. (1983). "A Structurational Analysis of Organizational Climate," in *Communication and Organizations: An Interpretive Approach,* L.L. Putnam and M.E. Pacanowsky (eds.). Beverly Hills, Calif.: Sage, pp. 195–219.

Poole, M.S., Seibold, D.R., and McPhee, R.D. (1985). "Group Decision-Making as a Structurational Process," *Quarterly Journal of Speech,* vol. 71, 74–102.

Putnam, L.L. (1983). "The Interpretive Perspective: An Alternative to Functionalism," in *Communication and Organizations: An Interpretive Approach,* L.L. Putnam and M.E. Pacanowsky (eds.). Beverly Hills, Calif.: Sage, pp. 31–53.

Putnam, L.L. and Pacanowsky, M.E. (eds.). (1983). *Communication and Organizations: An Interpretive Approach.* Beverly Hills, Calif.: Sage.

Radcliffe-Brown, A.R. (1965). *Structure and Function in Primitive Society.* New York: Free Press.

———. (1958). *Method in Social Anthropology.* Chicago: University of Chicago Press.

Rapoport, A. (1982). *The Meaning of the Built Environment.* Beverly Hills, Calif.: Sage.

———. (1966). "What Is Information?" in *Communication and Culture,* A.G. Smith (ed.). New York: Holt, Rinehart, and Winston, pp. 41–55.

Rawlins, W.K. (1983a). "Individual Responsibility in Relational Communication," in *Communications in Transition,* M.S. Mander (ed.). New York: Praeger, pp. 152–167.

———. (1983b). "Openness as Problematic in Ongoing Friendships: Two Conversational Dilemmas," *Communication Monographs,* vol. 50, 1–13.

Richards, A.I. (1939). *Land, Labor and Diet in Northern Rhodesia.* London: Oxford University Press.

Rommetveit, R. (1974). *On Message Structure.* London: John Wiley and Sons.

Rosen, L. (1984). *Bargaining for Reality: The Construction of Social Relations in a Muslim Community.* Chicago: University of Chicago Press.

Ruesch, J. and Bateson, G. (1951). *Communication: The Social Matrix.* New York: W.W. Norton and Company.

Sacks, H., Schegloff, E.A., and Jefferson, G. (1974). "A Simplest Systematics for the Organization of Turn-Taking for Conversation," *Language,* vol. 50, 696–735.

Sanders, R.E. (1983). "Tools for Cohering Discourse and Their Strategic Utilization: Markers of Structural Connections and Meaning Relations," in *Conversational Coherence,* R.T. Craig and K. Tracy (eds.). Beverly Hills, Calif.: Sage, pp. 67–80.

Scheflen, A.E. (1979). "On Communication Processes," in *Nonverbal Behavior: Applications and Cultural Implications,* A. Wolfgang (ed.). New York: Academic Press, pp. 1–16.

———. (1974). *How Behavior Means.* Garden City, N.Y.: Doubleday Anchor.

———. (1973). *Communicational Structure: Analysis of a Psychotherapy Transaction.* Bloomington, Ind.: Indiana University Press.

———. (1968). "Human Communication: Behavioral Programs and Their Integration in Interaction," *Behavioral Science,* vol. 13, 44–55.

———. (1965a). "The Bowl Gesture in the Whitaker-Malone Program" and "Variation in the Bowl Unit," in *Strategy and Structure in Psychotherapy, Behavioral Studies Monograph No. 2,* O.S. English (ed.). Philadelphia: Eastern Pennsylvania Psychiatric Institute, pp. 27–62.

———. (1965b). "Systems in Human Communication." Paper presented to the Society for General Systems Research, Berkeley, California.

Schenkein, J. (ed.). (1978). *Studies in the Organization of Conversational Interaction.* New York: Academic Press.

Schutz, A. and Luckmann, T. (1973). *The Structures of the Life-World.* Evanston, Ill.: Northwestern University Press.

Scott, R.L. (1977). "Communication as an Intentional Social System," *Human Communication Research,* vol. 3, 258–268.

Searle, J.R. (1969). *Speech Acts.* Cambridge: Cambridge University Press.

Shannon, C.E. and Weaver, W. (1949). *The Mathematical Theory of Communication.* Urbana, Ill.: University of Illinois Press.

Shimanoff, S. (1980). *Communication Rules.* Beverly Hills, Calif.: Sage.

Shotter, J. (1985). "Social Accountability and Self Specification," in *The Social Construction of the Person,* K.J. Gergen and K.E. Davis (eds.). New York: Springer-Verlag, pp. 167–189.

Shweder, R.A. and Miller, J.G. (1985). "The Social Construction of the Person: How Is It Possible?" in *The Social Construction of the Person,* K.J. Gergen and K.E. Davis (eds.). New York: Springer-Verlag, 41–69.

Sigman, S.J. (1986). "Adjustment to the Nursing Home as a Social Interactional Accomplishment," *Journal of Applied Communication Research,* vol. 14, 37–58.

———. (1985/86). "The Applicability of the Concept of Recruitment to the Communications Study of a Nursing Home: An Ethnographic Case Study," *International Journal of Aging and Human Development,* vol. 22, 215–233.

———. (1985a). "Some Common Mistakes Students Make When Learning Discourse Analysis," *Communication Education,* vol. 34, 119–127.

———. (1985b). "Conversational Behavior in Two Health Care Institutions for the Elderly," *International Journal of Aging and Human Development,* vol. 21, 137–154.

———. (1984). "Talk and Interaction Strategy in a Task-Oriented Group," *Small Group Behavior,* vol. 15, 33–51.

———. (1983a). "Some Multiple Constraints Placed on Conversational Topics," in *Conversational Coherence,* R.T. Craig and K. Tracy (eds.). Beverly Hills, Calif.: Sage, pp. 174–195.

———. (1983b). "Pets and Their Owners: A Pilot Ethnographic Study." Final grant report to the Gerontology Center, Institute for the Study of Human Development, Pennsylvania State University.

———. (1982). "Some Communicational Aspects of Patient Placement and Careers in Two Nursing Homes," unpublished Ph.D. dissertation, University of Pennsylvania.

———. (1981). "Some Notes on Conversational Fission," *Working Papers in Sociolinguistics,* No. 91. Austin: Southwest Educational Development Laboratory.

———. (1980a). "On Communication Rules from a Social Perspective," *Human Communication Research,* vol. 7, 37–51.

———. (1980b). "An Analysis of Conversational 'Fission' and 'Fusion.' " Paper presented to the American Anthropological Association, Washington, D.C.

Sigman, S.J. and Donnellon, A. (in press). "Discourse Rehearsal: Interaction Simulating Interaction," in *Communication and Simulation: From Two Fields to One Theme,* D. Crookall and D. Saunders (eds.). London: Multilingual Matters.

Sigman, S.J., Sullivan, S.J., and Wendell, M. (in press). "Conversation: Data Acquisition and Analysis," in *A Handbook for the Study of Human Communication: Methods and Instruments for Observing, Measuring, and Assessing Communication Processes,* C. Tardy (ed.). Norwood, N.J.: Ablex.

Sigman, S.J. and Wendell, M. (1986). "Strategic Questions and Fragmented Interaction in a Small Group," unpublished manuscript, State University of New York at Buffalo.

Simmel, G. (1949). "The Sociology of Sociability," *American Journal of Sociology,* vol. 55, pp. 254–261.

———. (1898). "The Persistence of Social Groups," *American Journal of Sociology,* vol. 3, 662–698.

Smircich, L. (1983). "Implications for Management Theory," in *Communication and Organizations: An Interpretive Approach,* L.L. Putnam and M.E. Pacanowsky (eds.). Beverly Hills, Calif.: Sage, pp. 221–241.

Sorokin, P.A. (1947). *Society, Culture, and Personality.* New York: Harper and Brothers.

Stokes, R. and Hewitt, J.P. (1976). "Aligning Actions," *American Sociological Review,* vol. 41, 838–849.

Strauss, A., Schatzman, L., Bucher, R., Ehrlich, D. and Sabshin, M. (1964). *Psychiatric Ideologies and Institutions.* New York: Free Press.

Stubbs, M. (1983). *Discourse Analysis: The Sociolinguistic Analysis of Natural Language.* Chicago: University of Chicago Press.

Thayer, L. (1972). "Communication Systems," in *The Relevance of General Systems Theory,* E. Laszlo (ed.). New York: George Braziller, pp. 93–121.

Thomas, S. (1980). "Some Problems of the Paradigm in Communication Theory," *Philosophy of Social Sciences,* vol. 10, 427–444.

Thompson, J.B. (1984). *Studies in the Theory of Ideology.* Berkeley: University of California Press.

Tracy, K. (1983). "Conversational Coherence: A Cognitively Grounded Rules Approach." Paper presented to the Speech Communication Association, Washington, D.C.

———. (1982). "The Issue-Event Distinction: A Rule of Conversation and Its Scope Conditions." Paper presented to the International Communication Association, Los Angeles.

Trager, G.L. and Smith, H.L., Jr. (1951). *An Outline of English Structure.* Norman, Okla.: Battenburg Press.

Trujillo, N. (1983). " 'Performing' Mintzberg's Roles: The Nature of Managerial Communication," in *Communication and Organizations: An Interpretive Approach,* L.L. Putnam and M.E. Pacanowsky (eds.). Beverly Hills, Calif.: Sage, pp. 73–97.

Turner, V. (1980). "Social Dramas and Stories about Them," *Critical Inquiry,* vol. 7, 141–168.

Van Dijk, T.A. (1983). "Discourse Analysis: Its Development and Application to the Structure of News," *Journal of Communication,* vol. 33, 20–43.

———. (1979). "Relevance Assignment in Discourse Comprehension," *Discourse Processes,* vol. 2, 113–126.

Van Gennep, A. (1960). *The Rites of Passage.* Chicago: University of Chicago Press.

Watzlawick, P., Beavin, J.H., and Jackson, D.D. (1967). *Pragmatics of Human Communication.* New York: W.W. Norton and Company.

Weick, K.E. (1983). "Organizational Communication: Toward a Research Agenda," *Communication and Organizations: An Interpretive Approach,* L.L. Putnam and M.E. Pacanowsky (eds.). Beverly Hills, Calif.: Sage, pp. 13–29.

Westley, B. and MacLean, M.J. (1957). "A Conceptual Model for Communication," *Journalism Quarterly,* vol. 34, 3–38.

Wiemann, J.M. and Knapp, M.L. (1975). "Turn-Taking in Conversations," *Journal of Communication,* vol. 25, 75–92.

Wilden, A. (1979). "Changing Frames of Order: Cybernetics and the *Machina Mundi,*" in *Communication and Control in Society,* K. Krippendorff (ed.). New York: Gordon and Breach Science Publishers, pp. 9–29.

Winch, P. (1958). *The Idea of a Social Science and Its Relation to Philosophy.* London: Routledge and Kegan Paul.

Winkin, Y. (ed.). (1980). *La Nouvelle Communication.* Paris: Editions du Seuil.

Worth, S. (1975). "Pictures Can't Say Ain't," *Versus,* vol. 12, 85–108.

Zabor, M. (1978). "Essaying Metacommunication: A Survey and Contextualization of Communication Research," unpublished Ph.D. dissertation, Indiana University.

Zerubavel, E. (1979). *Patterns of Time in Hospital Life: A Sociological Perspective.* Chicago: University of Chicago Press.

Index

About the Author

Stuart J. Sigman is on the faculty of the Department of Communication, State University of New York at Buffalo. He holds a doctorate in communication from the University of Pennsylvania. His papers have appeared in *Human Communication Research, Small Group Behavior, Working Papers in Sociolinguistics,* and the *International Journal of Aging and Human Development.*